ARTISTS IN CRIME

To my loving wife Margaret
and to our children
Jonathan, Mark and Jennifer

R.J.C.

For my mother, my brother
and the best of friends

B.P.

Artists in Crime

An illustrated survey of crime fiction first edition dustwrappers, 1920–1970

JOHN COOPER and B.A. PIKE

SCOLAR PRESS

Published by
SCOLAR PRESS
Gower House
Croft Road
Aldershot
Hants GU11 3HR
England

Ashgate Publishing Company
Old Post Road
Brookfield
Vermont 05036
USA

British Library Cataloguing-in-Publication data

Artists in Crime: Illustrated Survey of
Crime Fiction First Edition Dustwrappers,
1920–70
  I. Cooper, John II. Pike, B.A.
  741.640904

Library of Congress Cataloging-in-Publication Data

Cooper, John, 1944–
    Artists in crime: an illustrated survey of crime fiction first
  edition dustwrappers, 1920–1970/John Cooper and B.A. Pike.
      p.   cm.
    Includes bibliographical references and index.
    ISBN 1–85928–188–5
    1. Book jackets—History—20th century—Themes, motives.
  2. Detective and mystery stories—Illustrations.   I. Pike, B.A.
  II. Title.
  NC1882.C66   1995
  741.6′4′0904—dc20   95–14558
                          CIP
ISBN 1 85928 188 5

Typeset in Bembo by Bournemouth Colour Press and printed in Great Britain at the University Press, Cambridge

Contents

Acknowledgments

We are grateful to Jack Adrian and Richard Lancelyn Green, who gave us information about early dustwrappers. We acknowledge gratefully the collections from which some of the illustrations derive.

Introduction

Interest in the dustwrappers for twentieth-century crime fiction is intense among collectors. An important book with its wrapper is worth, in market terms, considerably more than the same book without the wrapper. An advertisement current in 1994 offered £3000 for a first edition in wrapper of Agatha Christie's first book. Anyone wanting simply to read that book or to own a copy of the text must find this beyond belief.

The reasons for such an offer have nothing to do with reading, since any printing of the text will serve the reader's purpose. They stem, rather, from the collector's needs, which are entirely different. Although the text is the essential reason why the book is interesting, it has no particular market value divorced from the mystique associated with the form in which it first appeared. As with anything rare and old and worth having, it is the object in its primary form that stirs the lust for possession. Reprints, like reproductions, are no substitute for originals.

Collectors of crime fiction first editions know from experience that many classic titles are rare even without their wrappers and no serious collector would reject a desirable early title because the wrapper was absent. None the less, we have perhaps reached the stage where collectors need to be reminded of the primary importance of the *books*. The wrappers are the icing on the cake.

In the earlier decades of the century, at least up to the Second World War, it appears to have been standard practice for readers, collectors and librarians to discard dustwrappers. In retrospect, this seems odd, since the visual appeal of the wrapper is often so much greater than that of the naked book. Anyone who owns a run of early Collins Crime Club titles without their wrappers will know the truth of this: they all look alike, with orange bindings and black capital lettering on their spines. The collector's desire to have the wrapper as well as the book makes perfect sense, provided dustwrapper worship does not take over, so that owning the wrapper becomes more important than owning the book. If a wrapper is desirable it must be, essentially, because the book for which it was produced is worth having.

That said, there can be no serious argument that a book in its wrapper is the natural focus of desire for the collector. In the context of collecting, with books as cultural artefacts worth owning and competing for, the wrapper completes the coveted object. It is desirable for several reasons: because it protects the binding; because the publisher may use it to communicate with the reader; or because its rarity increases the market value. Above and beyond all these, its visual appeal adds a new dimension to the pleasures of collecting mystery fiction.

Most crime fiction publishers in the period covered by this book acknowledge the importance of the dustwrapper as a visual adjunct to and enhancement of their books. The rare exceptions include Ernest Benn and, notoriously, Victor Gollancz, whose implacable yellow wrappers, unyielding through six decades, are devoid of visual appeal. The contrast between Gollancz and other publishers is easily demonstrated. He published Michael Innes, a major figure who suffered the indignity over fifty years of having every book he produced look exactly like all the others. Austin Lee, a minor figure, was published by Jonathan Cape, who employed Dick Hart, William McLaren, C.W. Bacon, Sax, Peter Curl, George Adamson and Stein to ensure that his books looked attractive.

Dustwrappers, as their name indicates, were originally provided by publishers to protect their books from dust and dirt, and they still serve this function. Alan Horne's introduction to *The Dictionary of Twentieth Century Book Illustrators* (Antique Collectors' Club 1994) states that the first dustwrapper was issued in 1833 and that the standard wrapper throughout the nineteenth century and well into the twentieth was a plain lettered cover. He also claims that pictorial wrappers did not become established until the 1920s.

There is, however, no doubt that publishers of crime fiction were putting their books into illustrated wrappers well before the 1920s. Newnes published Conan Doyle's *The Hound of the Baskervilles* in 1902 with an elaborately decorated cover and a grey dustwrapper. Both cover and wrapper feature a striking silhouette of the Hound on a moonlit skyline by A.G.J. (Alfred Garth Jones). In 1908 Eveleigh Nash published *The Luck of Norman Dale* by Barry Pain and James Blyth in a dustwrapper by Charles Pears with a drawing of a seaman aiming a crossbow at a fishing fleet. Guy Thorne's *The Socialist* appeared from Ward, Lock in 1909 with a three-colour illustration on its cream wrapper. Hodder & Stoughton issued A.E.W. Mason's *At the Villa Rose* in 1910 and a run of R. Austin Freeman's books from 1911, all with pictorial wrappers. Hickling's wrapper for E.C. Bentley's *Trent's Last Case*, published by Nelson in 1913, has the same illustration as the frontispiece, showing Mabel Manderson looking thoughtfully out to sea. Methuen published Ernest Bramah's first collection, *Max Carrados*, in 1914, with a pictorial wrapper illustrating the moment in 'The Game Played in the Dark' when Carrados turns the tables on his abductors. In 1915, Smith, Elder issued the last of the Sherlock Holmes novels, *The Valley of Fear*, with a pictorial wrapper showing a kneeling Holmes with the forearm of 'Jack Douglas'. Dudley Tennant's delightful wrapper for Freeman's *The Exploits of Danby Croker*, published by Duckworth in 1916, has Danby Croker and his double, one in evening dress, the other rifling a safe. John Murray published the penultimate Sherlock Holmes collection, *His Last Bow*, in 1917, with a wrapper by J. Abbey showing Holmes holding a white cockerel, such as was sacrificed by the mulatto cook at Wisteria Lodge.

By 1920 the pictorial wrapper was a standard feature of crime fiction both in first edition and reprinted form. Freeman's *A Savant's Vendetta*, J.S. Fletcher's *The Lost Mr. Linthwaite* and Agatha Christie's *The Mysterious Affair at Styles* all appeared in that year and their wrappers are reproduced in this book. The Christie title was published in New York in 1920, in London in 1921, each time with the same illustration by Alfred James Dewey. Other major titles for the year are *The Cask* by Freeman Wills Crofts, with a drawing by Lendon of a hand protruding from a cask, while sovereigns and sawdust fall from it to the floor; and H.C. Bailey's first collection, *Call Mr. Fortune*, which has an elegant drawing by Frank Wright for 'The Sleeping Companion', showing Birdie Bolton dead in an armchair, while her killer, knife in hand, disappears from view.

Many of the crime fiction wrappers of the 1920s are fully pictorial in an orthodox, representational manner, as for magazine illustration, which continued throughout the Golden Age of the inter-war years. John Campbell's illustrations for H.C. Bailey's Fortune stories in *The Windsor Magazine* and those by Jack Faulks for Margery Allingham's Campion stories in *The Strand Magazine* are two of the many distinguished graphic series produced at this time. In book form, however, crime fiction was seldom illustrated after the First World War, so that the dustwrapper offered the artists their only opportunity to contribute to the books that were published.

The work of Percy Graves is typical of the full pictorial style: witness his designs for G.D.H. Cole's *The Brooklyn Murders* and Agatha Christie's *The Secret of Chimneys*, each a meticulous rendering of a scene from the narrative. Ellen Edwards also illustrated the text, becoming in the process something of a specialist in damsels in distress (of whom the best known must be Mrs Ackroyd, shown rummaging guiltily on the wrapper for *The Murder of Roger Ackroyd*).

Frank Wright followed *Call Mr. Fortune* with equally attractive wrappers for *Mr. Fortune's Practice* and *Mr. Fortune's Trials*, again illustrating specific stories. The prolific Nick (later Nicolson) also contributed to the pictorial tradition: with his design for Philip MacDonald's *The Rasp*, showing Lucia Lemesurier kneeling in her bathing dress at the window of John Hoode's study; and with his wrapper for Anthony Wynne's *Sinners Go Secretly*, also with watchers at the window, anxious to know what is happening within. Frank Marston's wrapper for Ronald A. Knox's *The Footsteps at the Lock* is particularly choice, with its view over the Thames and full-length portrait of Nigel Burtell, his eyes slewed back towards the river and the hat floating on it. Equally appealing are Robb's view of *The House on Tollard Ridge* for this early Bles title by John Rhode and J. Morton-Sale's poetic view of the Coles's *The Man From the River*. Abbey's 1920s designs include two for John

Rhode: *The Ellerby Case*, with Sir Noel Ellerby lying dead beside his empty, open, green safe, and *Tragedy at 'The Unicorn'*, which has a splendid portrait of Dr Priestley. Youngman Carter began his career in the 1920s with wrappers for his wife's early novels, pictorial for *The White Cottage Mystery, The Crime at Black Dudley* and *Mystery Mile*. His later work is often more thematic and allusive, but whatever style he adopts his work is always distinguished.

In the midst of so much colour and variety the plain lettered wrappers for Ernest Benn's later titles appear dismal and niggardly indeed. E.R. Punshon's Carter and Bell novels and certain titles by S.S. Van Dine and J.J. Connington appeared with such wrappers. Yet even Benn's books were colourful earlier in the decade, as two novels by Connington admirably demonstrate: *Death at Swaythling Court* and *The Dangerfield Talisman*, the one clad in red, the other in yellow. In the same way, Victor Gollancz employed an artist at the outset of his career: E. McKnight Kauffer, no less. Eight of the books he published during 1928 had Kauffer wrappers with designs in muted colours and black, forming patterns rather than making direct pictorial statements and a long way from Abbey and Percy Graves. Two Connington novels have Kauffer wrappers: *Mystery at Lynden Sands* and *The Case with Nine Solutions*; so do Dorothy L. Sayers' *Lord Peter Views the Body* and Robert Milward Kennedy's *The Bleston Mystery*.

During the 1930s new names began to establish themselves. Leslie Stead was already in the field as early as 1924 – with his design for *The Templeton Case* by Victor L. Whitechurch – but he appears to have hit his stride in the 1930s, providing graceful drawings for books by R. Austin Freeman, Patricia Wentworth and R.A.J. Walling but also working much in the allusive style, setting a bold yellow spade on a blue background for Walling's *Bury Him Deeper*, for instance. Eugène Hastain's work is very appealing and contrives to be at once elegant and sinister. His designs for John Rhode's *Shot at Dawn*, Ethel Lina White's *Wax* and the early novels of Mary Fitt offer eloquent proof of this facility. V. Asta was also prolific at this time, designing for C. Daly King, John Rhode, the Coles and John Dickson Carr, among others. Asta has the dubious distinction of having provided the wrapper for Rhode's *The Venner Crime*, certainly the most common of all Golden Age detective novels in first edition. Bip Pares' wrappers for Ronald A. Knox range from the pictorial design of *The Body in the Silo* to the austere geometrical pattern of *Double Cross Purposes*. She also painted the victim of *A Bullet in the Ballet* and, a decade later, helped to launch Michael Gilbert on his distinguished career.

C.W. Bacon is unusual in that he continued to produce dustwrappers for crime fiction over several decades (like Nick and Youngman Carter, the latter perhaps holding the record for long service in the field). Bacon was designing for Patricia Wentworth in 1933 and for P.M. Hubbard in 1970. He was invariably stylish, whatever the mode in which he was working: thematic (as in Baynard Kendrick's *Death Knell* and Georgette Heyer's *Duplicate Death*); pictorial (John Dickson Carr's *The Nine Wrong Answers* and Christopher Bush's *The Case of the Burnt Bohemian*); or stylized (Herbert Brean's *Hardly a Man Is Now Alive*). He also drew impressive portraits of two well-regarded women detectives: Mrs Bradley (*Brazen Tongue*) and Miss Hogg (*Miss Hogg and the Bronte Murders*).

Broom Lynne came to prominence during the 1940s with his work for Macdonald, initially with the novels of Mary Fitt. All his designs for Macdonald and many that he produced later for Michael Joseph are inventive and visually stimulating. Freda Nichols also worked through the 1940s and 1950s, always effectively and sometimes arrestingly. She produced attractive wrappers for Craig Rice, Gladys Mitchell and Christianna Brand; and for *Death in Cranford* by the singleton writer Clara Stone, a novel of great charm with a wrapper to match. Denis McLoughlin worked mainly for Boardman, a publisher specializing in tough crime fiction, much of it American. The Bloodhound series ran through the 1950s and continued into the 1960s, still with McLoughlin as designer. Boardman also published Louisa Revell, a rare Bloodhound from the genteel tradition, for whom McLoughlin designed four striking wrappers.

B.S. (Val) Biro has at least one credit for the 1940s (*The Hollow Chest* by Alice Tilton) but he is chiefly celebrated among crime fiction collectors for his 1950s designs for John Dickson Carr (including splendid portraits of Dr Fell for *The Dead Man's Knock* and *A Dr. Fell Omnibus*) and for ten of the Carolus Deene series by Leo Bruce, in a fetching uniform style. Jarvis worked steadily for Hodder & Stoughton in the 1950s, designing in a range of styles for books by Delano Ames, Michael Gilbert and Patricia Wentworth (ten Miss Silver novels, including *The Gazebo*, which has a delightful wrapper). Sax is one of the most engaging of the post-war illustrators who worked in crime fiction wrapper design. Everything he touched he enhanced and his direct and detailed style served a number of authors particularly well: Pamela Branch, who was published by Hale, and such Hammond regulars as Margaret Erskine, Craig Rice and Guy Cullingford. The three designs he made for Margaret Erskine are hugely enticing and he knew exactly how to match visually the breezy bravura of Craig Rice.

Three other artists were especially prolific during the 1950s and 1960s: Kenneth Farnhill, William Randell and Stein. Farnhill's style is impossible to characterize, since he changes direction so often. His designs range from the allusive elegance of a series for Gladys Mitchell to the austerity of much of his Crime Club work (with Ngaio Marsh's *Clutch of Constables* as perhaps his least alluring work). Randell's style is emphatic and direct: he illustrates scenes and characters with unsubtle vigour. Occasionally he surpasses himself, as for Ellis Peters' *Death Mask*, a beautiful piece of work; but he can also sink to the level of *Vanity Dies Hard* for Ruth Rendell. Stein was very prolific and did much work for Macdonald. Many of his designs are dismayingly crude but at his best he is notably effective: in Gladys Mitchell's *Death and the Maiden*, for instance, or the three Blow and Manciple wrappers for Kenneth Hopkins. Some of his work is lamentable: Kathleen Freeman's *Gown and Shroud*, Douglas G. Browne's *Sergeant Death*, Carter Dickson's *Behind the Crimson Blind*.

Besides the regular, prolific dustwrapper artists, a considerable number of designers and illustrators made occasional forays into crime fiction design. Some particularly distinguished names figure on the roster: Edward Ardizzone, Nicolas Bentley, Edward Bawden, Eric Fraser, C. Walter Hodges, Philip Gough. Ardizzone produced three characteristic designs for Cyril Hare: the first editions of *An English Murder* and *That Yew Tree's Shade* and a reissue of *Tragedy at Law*, of which the original wrapper is distressingly plain. Nicolas Bentley provided the wrappers for the two 'Peter Antony' novels by the Shaffer twins, both with exuberant portraits of Mr Verity, their detective. He also illustrated the earlier title, *The Woman in the Wardrobe*, with a series of portraits of the characters. Edward Bawden's wrapper for Eric Linklater's *Mr. Byculla* is apt and telling. Fraser, Hodges and Gough are represented here.

Many other artists deserve a mention, however fleeting: Joan Kiddell Monroe, whose designs for four of Josephine Bell's novels are especially pleasing; Felix Kelly and Victor Reinganum, both employed by Faber for novels by Cyril Hare, who was remarkably fortunate in his designers; Ionicus, whose picture of the bookshop in Edward Grierson's *A Crime of One's Own* is very appealing; Timothy Birdsall, designer for Dorothy Salisbury Davis' *Old Sinners Never Die*, matching the author's verbal portrait of General Jarvis with a delightful drawing of him; Olga Lehmann, whose eerie design for *Dead Lion* by the Bonetts catches the essence of its action; William Stobbs, who illustrated Christianna Brand's children's mystery, *Welcome to Danger*, and designed the colourful wrapper for Thomas Kyd's *Blood of Vintage*; and Charles Mozley and Errol Le Cain, both of whom made striking pictures for works by P.D. James. Dick Hart, S.G. Hulme Beaman, Leslie Wood, Fritz Wegner, Jack Matthew and Denys Watkins-Pitchford are also represented here.

A few American artists also feature in this book: Vera Bock, Leo Manso and Charles Lofgren among them. That they are so few is no reflection on them. It merely means that we have had access to far fewer American wrappers than to British ones.

Since the 1960s the art of the crime fiction dustwrapper has been allowed to wither and die. There is the occasional honourable exception but, by and large, the photographer took over from the graphic artist and we were the poorer in consequence. Throughout the 1970s and 1980s the chief publishers of crime fiction employed photographers in a successful attempt to make every book look much the same as its stablemates. The main exception was Victor Gollancz, the firm that did not use artists either.★

The present book is intended as a tribute to the artists represented and as a celebration and record of their achievement. It is sad that so many designs are unattributed, since so often this prevents credit being given where it is due.

B.A. Pike

★It is fair to Gollancz to say that some attempts were made to improve the visual aspect of the firm's dustwrappers during the later 1980s. At the beginning of the 1990s fully pictorial wrappers were introduced.

1
Damsels in Distress

The White Rider

LESLIE CHARTERIS

Ward, Lock 1928
artist: **Abbey**

Leslie Charteris is famous for creating
Simon Templar, otherwise known as 'The
Saint'. The hero of his first two novels,
written in the late 1920s, is William
Kennedy, Assistant Commissioner of
Police for the Metropolis. In *The White
Rider*, he investigates when Marion Fenton
is kidnapped and held to ransom by a
transatlantic villain. She alone knows
where to find the million pounds left by
her stepfather, Bernard Seldon, who has
come to a violent end. Abbey's wrapper
shows the distressed Marion, in a green
suit and white blouse, lying on a bed while
Peter Lestrange, 'with bruised, torn fingers
wrestled with the ropes about her'.

Other Man's Danger

MAXWELL MARCH

Collins 1933
artist: **unknown**

Other Man's Danger is the first of three
spirited thrillers by Margery Allingham, all
serialized in 'Answers' in her own name
but issued in book form under the
pseudonym 'Maxwell March'. The action
centres on Jennifer Fern, the 'Tragic
Heiress', whose fiancés come invariably to
a sticky end, so that she remains unmarried
despite great riches and 'true beauty'.
Robin Grey, the man of 'dangerous
secrets', witnesses the latest attempt to
eliminate a suitor and is soon involved in
her fight against the 'terrible scourge' that
'brings death to any man' who seeks to
marry her. The yellow wrapper has a dark
blue diagonal band against which 'the calm
tranquil loveliness' of Jennifer's face shows
up bravely. Wielding a hypodermic needle
in the corner is the sinister Dr Crupiner.

The Empty Bed
HERBERT ADAMS

Methuen 1928
artist: **Frank Marston**

Herbert Adams wrote 51 crime novels over a period of 34 years, many of them excellent examples of the traditional detective story. In *The Empty Bed*, Silas Gurney's relations are spending Christmas with him. When he is found dead on Christmas Eve, it is Joyce Gurney, his niece, who sends for barrister Jimmie Haswell to assist the police to discover the murderer. Frank Marston's design shows Joyce in her red outfit with a black and green hat. She describes the scene to Jimmie Haswell: 'I was carrying my shoes and was just going to open the door when I heard that awful scream. I was terrified.'

The Footsteps that Stopped
A. FIELDING

Collins 1926
artist: **C. Morse**

A. Fielding wrote 25 detective novels, many of which are ponderous and unconvincing. All but two are cases for Chief-Inspector Pointer of Scotland Yard. In *The Footsteps that Stopped* no clues appear to have been left by the murderer of Mrs Tangye, so that Pointer – and the reader – must rely purely on deductive reasoning to solve the case. C. Morse's design shows Barbara Ash wearing purple trimmed with black fur and in a matching hat. Olive, her maid, stands behind. Both women gaze upwards in horror, Barbara gasping 'What's the matter?' and Olive replying: 'The footsteps! The footsteps that stopped! They've stopped again on the landing above us. I smelled death! They're coming in! … They're coming for us!'

The Case of the Green Felt Hat

CHRISTOPHER BUSH

Cassell 1939
artist: **James E. McConnell**

The Case of the Green Felt Hat has Ludovic and Bernice Travers on their honeymoon near Pettistone, the village to which the convicted swindler, Harley Brewse, has retired after his years in prison. When Brewse is found dead, his green felt hat is missing; and its eventual discovery elsewhere is a cause of much confusion. Only when the significance of its position is established is the case closed. Molly Pernaby is one of several with a grudge against Brewse. McConnell shows her looking tense in an orange coat, kneeling 'in the wood not far back from the road', as if placing or removing the hat.

The Woman in Red

ANTHONY GILBERT

Collins Crime Club 1941
artist: **Leslie Stead**

Anthony Gilbert's books are noted for vigorous characterization and adroit plotting. *The Woman in Red* is charged with atmosphere from the first page. As soon as she accepts the position of secretary-companion to Mrs Ponsonby, Julia Ross knows there is something very wrong about the old lady, who always wears red: 'why should she suddenly think of blood, that was red, too?' 'That first night she began to traverse the path of understanding the appalling thing Mrs Ponsonby meant to do.' Stead shows Julia being 'awakened by someone violently rattling the door handle'. When the notice of her death appears, her friend, Colin Bruce, determines to investigate with the help of Arthur Crook.

The Murder of Roger Ackroyd

AGATHA CHRISTIE

Collins 1926
artist: **Ellen Edwards**

Agatha Christie, justly the most famous of detective writers, created some of the most ingenious plots in the history of the genre. The denouement in *The Murder of Roger Ackroyd*, the third Hercule Poirot novel, caused a public outcry when the book was first published. Ellen Edwards' design has Mrs Ackroyd, looking nervous in a dark pink dress, searching the drawers of her brother-in-law's desk for his will. Ackroyd has been 'a peculiar man over money matters' and she hopes the will might enable her to take care of unpaid bills. She has earlier been wondering 'if Roger keeps his will in one of the drawers of the desk'.

Fear by Night

PATRICIA WENTWORTH

Hodder & Stoughton 1934
artist: **Leslie Stead**

Fear by Night is one of Patricia Wentworth's romantic adventure stories, set this time by Loch Dhu, which seems to be inhabited by a mysterious monster. Because Ann Vernon is to be the chief beneficiary of the will of wealthy Elias Paulett, she becomes the target of a murder plot. Charles Anstruther is in love with her and they are both caught up in mysterious events on a small Scottish island. Stead's wrapper is blue, green, black and white and shows Ann as she crouches 'in the bottom of the copper' and hears 'the clatter of the lantern on the floor and the footsteps of the men coming up into the wash-house. They were coming up out of that hole in the floor.'

Murder in the Basement

ANTHONY BERKELEY

Hodder & Stoughton 1932
artist: **unknown**

Anthony Berkeley's *Murder in the Basement* begins with Reginald and Molly Dane, recently returned from honeymoon, moving into their 'semi-detached messuage'. In the cellar, with 'the cobwebs hanging from every available projection', Reginald uses a pickaxe to investigate a curious depression in a corner of the floor. Molly, dressed in dark green, moves back in horror as her husband warns her 'there's something pretty beastly here'. Chief-Inspector Moresby calls upon Roger Sheringham to help identify the body exhumed from the basement, believing it to be that of a young woman last heard of at the preparatory school where Roger had held a temporary post.

The Murder of an Old Man

DAVID FROME

Methuen 1929
artist: **unknown**

The Murder of an Old Man is the second of Zenith Brown's novels, written as 'David Frome' before the launching of her 'Leslie Ford' pseudonym. It precedes the Pinkerton-Bull series and features Major Gregory Lewis, ex-MP and 'inquiry agent for the upper classes'. Here he investigates the murder of millionaire John Carter Cunningham, shot dead at his home, Ashingdene Manor. The handsome wrapper shows the 'circular staircase of graceful wrought-iron' ascending from the library. Moving furtively at the top is Sir Coburn Reynolds, grasping the papers he has removed from Cunningham's safe. From below, his daughter Joan looks up anxiously.

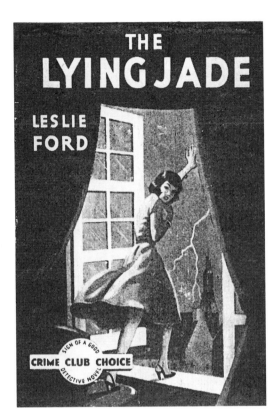

The Lying Jade
LESLIE FORD

Collins Crime Club 1953
artist: **unknown**

The Lying Jade is the last of the Primrose-
Latham novels and is set in Washington at
the time of the McCarthy hearings. Rufus
Brent was to have headed the Industrial
Techniques Commission but has quit for
'purely personal and private reasons'. He
becomes the victim of a vicious
persecution, organized and orchestrated by
a hostile congressman, determined to bring
him down. Brent's daughter Molly is also
undermined by her father's enemy, to the
point where she is driven to attempt
suicide. The artist shows her 'at the
opened window' high in Grace Latham's
house, lit by 'monstrous flashes' of
lightning 'as she stood … trying blindly to
run'.

The Dower House Mystery
PATRICIA WENTWORTH

Hodder & Stoughton 1925
artist: **unknown**

In several of her earlier works, Patricia
Wentworth draws on the theme of the
damsel in distress. In *The Dower House
Mystery*, Annabel Grey, a charming widow,
accepts the offer of the Dower House,
which she had visited in her girlhood. She
has no idea, however, that a number of
previous tenants had left hurriedly after a
few days. Strange noises are heard;
unpleasant happenings occur. Jane Smith,
her uncle, Cornelius Molloy, and Julian Le
Mesurier, or 'Piggy', Chief of the Criminal
Investigation Department, assist in
unravelling the mystery. Dominating the
wrapper, over the Dower House, is 'a
plain, ordinary ghost. A lady in 'er night-
dress, with 'er 'air down 'er back'. She is
the unhappy spirit of the house.

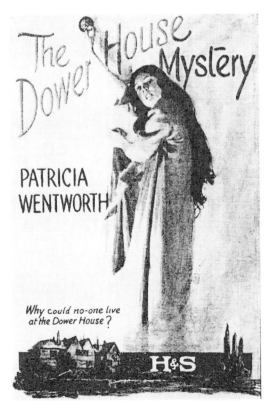

Death's Dateless Night

THURMAN WARRINER

Hodder & Stoughton 1952
artist: **unknown**

Death's Dateless Night is the third case for
Mr Ambo and the Archdeacon,
encountered while they are 'travelling …
on a tour of the Basses Alpes'. Lucia
Calvin lives at Pont du Verdom with her
elderly, ailing husband, who is 'being
persecuted in a most appalling fashion'. He
is also recognized as a famous impresario,
officially dead and buried some years
earlier. The mystery is resolved in
England, where John Scotter's help is
enlisted. The romantic wrapper shows
Lucia looking apprehensive before her
home in Pont du Verdom, the former
'hotel de Dieu'. The image is in the spirit
of the text rather than to the letter: the
house is not raised in isolation but has
'cliffs immediately above and behind'.

AN ENTIRELY NEW NOVEL 7/3 net

Death's Dateless Night

THURMAN WARRINER

An H & S 'Crime' Choice—Chosen for Enjoyment

Guest in the House

PHILIP MACDONALD

Doubleday Crime Club 1955
artist: **Joan Cummings**

The *Guest in the House* in Philip
MacDonald's suspense novel is Colonel
Ivor St George, an Englishman visiting
California, where he is staying with an old
friend, Jeff Gould, and his wife Mary. He
is disturbed by the unhappy atmosphere in
their home. One afternoon, the cause of
the trouble calls in person at the house.
Joan Cumming's green and blue wrapper
shows the unhappy Mary Gould looking
towards the black figure of her former
husband, Victor Voss, framed in the french
window. Once again he has returned,
demanding more money, constantly
bleeding the Goulds, so that they never
have any resources. The artist conveys
Mary's 'sick, jarring feeling as she heard his
voice' and her wish that 'she didn't feel so
frightened'.

Philip MacDonald

GUEST
IN THE
HOUSE

CRIME CLUB SELECTION

Farewell Crown and Good-Bye King
MARGOT BENNETT

Eyre & Spottiswoode 1953
artist: **unknown**

Margot Bennett, who, to quote Anthony Berkeley Cox, was 'one of the brightest stars in the crime-fiction firmament', wrote six detective novels, all witty, with good characterization and intricate plots. In *Farewell Crown and Good-Bye King* the 'tall and darkly slender' Kate Browning, wearing 'a small grey felt hat', is trying to locate Louis Fernak. Very afraid, she walks away from the unpleasant 'square stone house' in Sussex. She imagines the loathsome, grinning Dr Jaseowicz scurrying after her through the garden, 'with its wall of sweet black trees riding up to the sky with their cargo of rooks'.

Or Be He Dead
JAMES BYROM

Chatto & Windus 1958
artist: **Dick Hart**

Or Be He Dead is the first of James Byrom's three distinctive detective novels and harks back to a celebrated criminal trial in the 1890s. Dick Hart shows the Parisian prostitute Marcelline under threat from the true-crime writer Raymond Kennington, who wants some information from her. The gun is an air-pistol hired for the occasion, but it serves its purpose: inured to 'threatening males', Marcelline comes across with what she knows. Her posture exactly mirrors the text, even to the slight turn of her head 'a little sideways'. The background is orange, the drawing black and white.

The Poisoned Chocolates Case

ANTHONY BERKELEY

Collins 1929
artist: **Napoli**

Anthony Berkeley wrote several outstanding detective novels, among them *The Poisoned Chocolates Case*. The doomed Joan Bendix is shown by Napoli in a blue petticoat, looking horrified as a hand drips poison from a green bottle onto a box of chocolates. The box has been sent to Sir Eustace Pennefather at his club and is there given to Graham Bendix, who takes it home to his wife. As she eats the contents, she comments that 'they are really strong', 'they almost burn' and 'one tasted far too strongly of almonds'. Her death sets the police a baffling problem, taken by Roger Sheringham to the small Crime Circle of which he is president. Each of the six members, including Ambrose Chitterwick, supplies a different solution. [See colour section, page (a).]

The House of the Arrow

A.E.W. MASON

Hodder & Stoughton n.d. (1924)
artist: **unknown**

The House of the Arrow is the famous book in which Inspector Hanaud tells Jim Frobisher that 'Blackmail's an ugly word'. The volatile 'great man' of the Sûreté here investigates a sinister affair in Dijon, 14 years on from *At the Villa Rose*, in which A.E.W. Mason introduced him. The wrapper shows Ann Upcott in 'the extremity of her horror' at betrayal and the imminent threat of death: 'her face spoke for her. Her upper lip was drawn back a little from her teeth and there was a look in her eyes which appalled Jim Frobisher outside the door'. Hanaud is there, too, of course: and Ann survives her ordeal. [See colour section, page (a).]

The Magic Casket

R. AUSTIN FREEMAN

Hodder & Stoughton 1927
artist: **unknown**

The colourful wrapper of R. Austin Freeman's *The Magic Casket* is blue, green, red and white. It shows an 'ordinary Japanese casket in the form of a squat, shapeless figure', found by Dr Thorndyke in an abandoned bag belonging to Miss Mabel Bonney. The pearls draped round the casket have been stolen from her family previously. The casket is sought by a Japanese gang who have killed Mabel's father. Understandably, Mabel, 'a lady to her finger tips', is shown glancing nervously over her shoulder as she is 'still haunted by Japanese'. Dr Thorndyke uses his powers of observation and his ingenuity to solve the mystery of the casket and recover the pearls in the first of the nine stories in the collection. [See colour section, page (a).]

The Box Office Murders

FREEMAN WILLS CROFTS

Collins 1929
artist: **unknown**

Freeman Wills Crofts was one of the first writers to use police procedure methodically. He created one of the greatest police detectives, Inspector Joseph French, whose investigations cover 30 novels. In *The Box Office Murders*, three girls working in the box-offices of various London cinemas are murdered. Molly Moran, employed in the box-office of the Panopticon, is cajoled by French into assisting in solving the case. Style, one of the three villains involved, discovers this and kidnaps her: 'Molly couldn't speak. She felt too sick with horror. She lay gazing up at that narrow face with its evil, staring eyes and its expression of almost maniac hate.' The scene is overseen by a portrait head of Inspector French. [See colour section, page (a).]

2
Distraught Men

The Chief Witness

HERBERT ADAMS

Collins Crime Club 1940
artist: **unknown**

The Chief Witness is the ninth case of
amateur detective Roger Bennion to be
recorded by Herbert Adams. Roger is
'dark, clean shaven, in the early thirties'
and loves action. The deaths of two
brothers in similar circumstances and at the
same moment, though in different places,
indicate a suicide pact, but Roger finds
that they have been murdered. Having
been drugged and captured by the
murderer, he awakes to find himself stark
naked and 'tied in a sort of invalid chair':
'There were cords round his waist and his
neck, knotted to the iron framework at the
back. A handkerchief stuffed into his
mouth prevented his uttering a sound.'

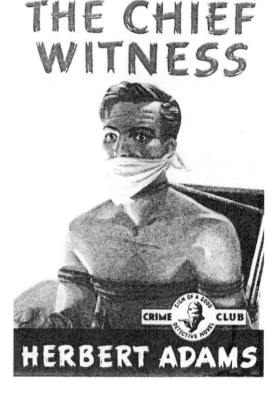

John Brand's Will

HERBERT ADAMS

Methuen 1933
artist: **Abbey**

Herbert Adams devised an intricate plot
for *John Brand's Will*, in which Susan
Heriot, Brand's adopted daughter, tries to
reconcile him with his brother George.
Later, after returning from abroad, Susan
finds that they were reunited, but her
father has died and everything has been left
to George and his children, so that she is
now homeless. Robert Onslow, the son of
her solicitor, is suspicious and investigates.
Abbey's fine, detailed wrapper shows the
captured Robert in the library at Varnoll,
'in a chair, bound hand and foot', with
part of the contested will in the
background. One of his captors is berating
him: 'As she spoke she bent forward and
struck him cruelly on the face with her
open hand.'

The Beach of Atonement

ARTHUR W. UPFIELD

Hutchinson 1930
artist: **Robb**

The Beach of Atonement is one of the four Arthur Upfield novels that do not feature Detective-Inspector Napoleon Bonaparte. Like the Boney novels, it is set in Australia. Robb's wrapper shows a forlorn Arnold Dudley sitting on a rock on Atonement beach, with green waves crashing onto golden sand. He has murdered his wife's lover, Edmund Tracy, and his mind continues to be obsessed by him: 'Hour after hour he sat, his face cupped in his hands.' He reacts with 'an unpleasant nervous start' when approached by the 'slim figure of a young woman of some twenty years of age', who has come to ask his help. The artist shows her as a ghostly figure, contributing to the melancholy of the scene.

Beggar's Choice

PATRICIA WENTWORTH

Hodder & Stoughton 1930
artist: **Norah Schlegel**

For Patricia Wentworth's *Beggar's Choice*, Norah Schlegel depicts Carthen Fairfax, sitting on a park bench and gazing at his boots. A torn handbill offering £500 lies across the top right-hand corner. The book provides different viewpoints, as it offers extracts from Fairfax's diary interspersed with conventional narrative and letters. Fairfax is down on his luck: he 'looked bored, but behind the boredom there was distress and distaste'. 'It was a muggy day … but even without the sun to show them up' his boots give him 'a sick, discouraged sort of feeling'. When he meets Isobel, an old friend, his luck changes but the route to happiness is not without incident or danger.

Fatality in Fleet Street

C. ST JOHN SPRIGG

Eldon 1933
artist: **Chesney**

Fatality in Fleet Street is the second of the
seven crime novels of C. St John Sprigg.
Chesney's mainly grey design portrays a
tense and worried Lord Carpenter,
governing director of Affiliated
Publications. 'His famous Napoleonesque
profile with the wandering lock of hair on
the high brow' is clearly visible as he
telephones. For 12 months he has been
propounding in *The Mercury* the idea that
'Russia must be crushed' and that Britain
'should be the executioner'; but this desire
to declare war on Russia is abhorred by
the government and the newspaper staff.
When Carpenter is found stabbed in his
suite at *The Mercury* it is the paper's crime
expert, Charles Venables, who assists the
police in revealing the murderer.

The Room with the Iron Shutters

ANTHONY WYNNE

Hutchinson n.d. (1929)
artist: **Nick**

The Room with the Iron Shutters is a locked
room mystery for Dr Hailey, Harley Street
consultant and 'amateur in the study of
crime'. Lord Gerald Glen is observed
through a window in his study at Shawdon
Hall, 'in distress of some sort', as Nick so
expressively shows. Minutes later he lies
'stabbed through the heart' in the locked
and shuttered room, with the windows
'bolted on the inside'. Beside him is 'a
sheet of note-paper' with the scrawled
message 'I have been murdered'. There are
'no footprints anywhere' and nothing
suggests 'that any struggle took place'.
'The murderer can't have been hidden in
the chimney', there are no 'secret
chambers and passages' and the weapon is
nowhere to be found.

Crime of Violence
RUFUS KING

Methuen 1938
artist: **G.P. Micklewright**

Crime of Violence is the penultimate case of Lieutenant Valcour of the New York police, whose eventful recorded career spans the decade from 1929 to 1939. Here he investigates the sudden death of Horace Worthington, found shot, with the gun beside him, in the New York home of his prospective mother-in-law, which is closed for the season. Micklewright's powerful portrait gets his features exactly right, recording impeccably the 'importantly jowled face' with its 'piglike little eyes' and 'sensual lips, thick and flat and damp-looking'. He fails, however, to take into account the 'cadaveric spasm' which has left him looking 'pleased about something, expectant, as if something nice were going to happen'.

The Bell of Death
ANTHONY GILBERT

Collins Crime Club 1939
artist: **unknown**

The Bell of Death is the sixth investigation created for Arthur Crook and his able assistant, Bill Parsons, by Anthony Gilbert (Lucy Beatrice Malleson). The Reverend Henry Fane, Vicar of St Ethelburga's, discovers a body in the belfry: 'They went to ring the bell for morning service and there he was all tangled up in the rope.' The wrapper shows the bell of St Ethelburga's and the victim, 'Hoover-face' Harvey, with his hands over his ears, both against a yellow background. William Ferris, who looks after the church interior, disappears and his wife calls in Arthur Crook to find him.

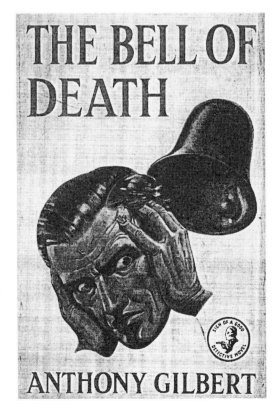

A Silver Spade

LOUISA REVELL

Boardman 1950
artist: **Denis McLoughlin**

A Silver Spade is the third of Louisa
Revell's stylish novels, all with Julia Tyler
of Rossville, Virginia. It is set at Camp
Pirate Island, a summer school for
exceptionally clever girls in Casco Bay,
Maine. Miss Julia joins the school as its
substitute Latin teacher, persuaded less by
'salary and scenery and fine salt air' than
the fact that anonymous letters have
appeared in the community. McLoughlin
shows a dramatic example of the 'free-
lance digging' undertaken at different
times on Pirate Island, whether by children
prospecting for pieces of eight, teachers
seeking Indian artefacts or a desperate man,
burying a body 'in a hurry, just plain,
without a coffin or a shroud'.

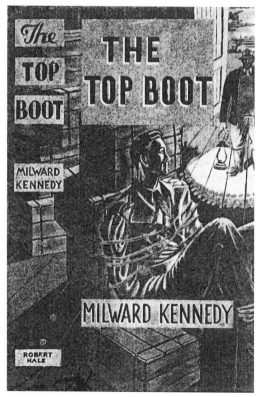

The Top Boot

MILWARD KENNEDY

Hale 1950
artist: **Brinklow**

The Top Boot is the penultimate novel of
Milward Kennedy, who began with formal
detection but turned increasingly to the
thriller in his later years. Henri Brown is a
Canadian mountie over in England on a
trail that takes him from the Top Boot, a
West End nightclub, to the village of
Penfold in Sussex. Brinklow's striking
wrapper shows him in a barn, bound hand
and foot after being laid out. Confronting
him is a man in 'big rubber wellingtons'
and 'rough pants', with 'a hat of some kind
low over his eyes'. He is 'carrying an oil
lamp, hanging low and with a metallic
shade above it'.

New People at The Hollies

JOSEPHINE BELL

Hodder & Stoughton 1961
artist: **Auguste von Briesen**

New People at The Hollies is a sinister novel about the abuse of elderly people in a provincial nursing-home. Miss Tindall and her assistant are not the calm, kindly, competent women who traditionally run such places. They appear to be acting the part, as, indeed, they are. Mr Coltman is an ex-policeman, whose habitual vigilance is a danger to them, but as he moves nearer to the truth he puts himself increasingly at risk: 'he felt a sudden chill and knew that he was afraid'. Von Briesen's dramatic wrapper shows him at bay in the garden of The Hollies. It is appropriately bleak: grey, purple and white.

Fantasy and Fugue

ROY FULLER

Verschoyle 1954
artist: **Alan Lindsay**

Fantasy and Fugue is a fraught first-person narrative set in literary London, with a publisher as narrator and a writer as victim. Like Albert Campion in *Traitor's Purse*, Harry Sinton is amnesiac and must discover his own actions and motives as well as those of the others involved. Alan Lindsay's potent wrapper displays his constant neurotic fear that he may himself be the killer, his 'long-held belief that all [he] could arouse was fear and repugnance'. Within his bowler lies the body of Max Callis, with Chelsea Bridge and the Thames embankment as a backdrop.

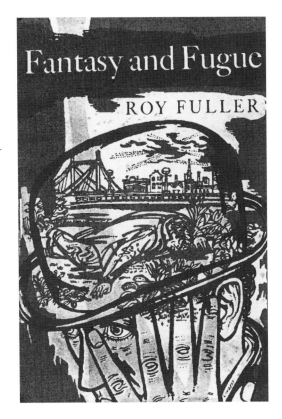

The First Time He Died

ETHEL LINA WHITE

Collins 1935
artist: **Youngman Carter**

'The first time Charles Baxter died he was not buried.' Not wishing to work, Baxter has decided to insure his life and then conveniently 'die' in order to claim the proceeds. In *The First Time He Died*, Ethel Lina White provides a fascinating study of an insecure, inadequate man, shown in blue and brown by Youngman Carter against a maroon and orange background. He has 'a dark bearded face with liquid brown eyes' and peers out nervously from between curtains while clasping 'a chaplet of bay leaves', sent as a wreath by his unsuspecting sister. The fraud is successful but he is constantly in fear of betrayal and imprisonment. In his imagination, prison bars overlay the curtains through which he is peering.

The Perennial Boarder

PHOEBE ATWOOD TAYLOR

Collins Crime Club 1942
artist: **Leslie Stead**

The Perennial Boarder is Miss Olive Beadle, who has for 29 years been spending her summers at the Whelk Inn at Quisset on Cape Cod. Shortly after arriving for her 30th annual holiday her body is found at the deserted inn by Asey Mayo and his cousin Jennie, who have come to deliver clams. Later, it is established that Miss Beadle is not the victim: the corpse is simply wearing her clothes. Stead shows the moment after Asey has grabbed 'up the candelabrum from the mantelpiece ... held it high and strode over beside her'. His alarmed expression is understandable: Jennie's scream has 'split his ear-drums'.

Patrick Butler for the Defence

JOHN DICKSON CARR

Hamish Hamilton 1956
artist: **C.W. Bacon**

John Dickson Carr's books are always entertaining, with strong atmosphere and brilliant plots. For *Patrick Butler for the Defence*, C.W. Bacon's design is pervaded by 'the soft, clammy, ghost-white' fog in Lincoln's Inn Fields on 'an afternoon late in November'. Abu of Ispahan, looking distraught and seeming 'bulkier by reason of a long, dark, rather shabby overcoat with an astrakhan collar', seeks the solicitors Prentice, Prentice and Vaughan. 'On his head, a little sideways, he wore the green fez, with tassel.' Shortly after his meeting with Hugh Prentice, Abu is stabbed to death, practically under Hugh's eye. Prentice resolves to enlist the help of barrister Patrick Butler in solving the murder and, if necessary, acting in his defence.

Dishonour among Thieves

E.C.R. LORAC

Collins Crime Club 1959
artist: **William Randell**

Two pseudonyms were used by Edith Caroline Rivett: E.C.R. Lorac and Carol Carnac. *Dishonour among Thieves* is the last of 58 well-crafted detective novels written as by E.C.R. Lorac. For the last time the author returns to the fell country of Lunesdale in Lancashire, where Chief-Inspector Robert Macdonald has a farm to which he hopes to retire. When a dead body is discovered in a deserted house nearby, Macdonald's investigation becomes linked to the escape of a prisoner from Dartmoor. William Randell's atmospheric grey-blue design shows Rory Macshane, wearing a raincoat to hide his prison uniform and carrying the sack containing 'his meagre store of hoarded food packed in two tins', as he flees through the dense Dartmoor mist.

The Death of a Millionaire

G.D.H. AND M. COLE

Collins 1925
artist: **Ellen Edwards**

The Death of a Millionaire is the first acknowledged collaboration between the Coles, despite the blurb, which gives it to G.D.H. Cole alone. The eponymous victim is Hugh Radlett, who disappears from Sugden's Hotel in London, supposedly murdered by his secretary and removed in a trunk. His room is found in total disarray, with bloodstains on the bed and one of the walls and, in the wardrobe, 'a human form, gagged and bound, hand and foot', 'struggling violently … and making frantic efforts to speak through his gag'. Ellen Edwards shows Alfred Culpepper 'in his tight bonds' with, beyond him, a reward poster and the silhouette of his daughter, the devious and enigmatic Norah.

THE DEATH OF A MILLIONAIRE

G.D.H.
and
MARGARET COLE

£10,000
REWARD

By the authors of 'The Brooklyn Murders'

Slocombe Dies

L.A.G. STRONG

Collins Crime Club 1942
artist: **Hof**

Slocombe Dies is the first of L.A.G. Strong's crime novels, different in kind from the whodunits that followed it. It undertakes to explain 'how the crime came to be committed' and opens with two friends driving on a Dartmoor road and happening on two men, one dead, with a 'hideous, bloody depression under [his] thin reddish hair', the other untying the ropes that bind him. The rest of the narrative is retrospective and demonstrates exactly how this encounter came about. Hof's wrapper, in pink and green washes, shows Charlie Bird with 'a sulky, defiant expression' on his face and Sam Slocombe advancing towards him, 'stark mad' and brandishing a revolver.

A Touch of Drama

GUY CULLINGFORD

Hammond 1960
artist: **Sax**

A Touch of Drama is a suspense novel about a successful West End dramatist whose wife disappears while he is revisiting his home town after many years away. The word 'murderer' appears in lipstick on her mirror and he is suspected of having killed her. Rumours proliferate and public feeling mounts against him until, on the opening night of his new play, the audience stops the performance and vents its hostility: 'They began to hiss and boo and stamp their feet ... In the stalls people rose in their seats ... a woman screamed ... "What have you done with your wife, you devil?"'. Sax records the moment with characteristic vigour.

Footsteps Behind Me

ANTHONY GILBERT

Collins Crime Club 1953
artist: **unknown**

Anthony Gilbert was a reliable and very popular writer right through the Golden Age into the early 1970s. In *Footsteps Behind Me*, Edward (Teddy) Lane has sunk to the level of blackmail. What he has not anticipated is that others are more ruthless than he is and that someone is trying to murder him. On the wrapper, a worried Teddy Lane wipes his sweating face as a mysterious figure watches from across the road: 'He crossed the road shakily and went down the cul-de-sac ... expecting at every instant that some dark figure would leap out of the blackness and bear him to the ground.' Later, he is indeed murdered and Arthur Crook is hired to prove that one of his blackmail victims is not the murderer.

Garstons

H.C. BAILEY

Methuen 1930
artist: **G.W. Goss**

Garstons is the first of H.C. Bailey's
detective novels and marks the first
appearance of the wily solicitor, Joshua
Clunk. Mrs Garston, the mother of the
great ironmaster, Lord Croyland, dies
mysteriously in the night at Bradstock
Abbey. G.W. Goss shows her lying at the
feet of her son, illumined by May Dean's
torch, 'piercing into the gloom'. Lord
Croyland is 'still in his evening clothes'
and looks forgivably rattled 'under the
white glare' of the torch-beam.
Superintendent Bell wonders why the old
lady should die 'in the one place where
the lamp didn't work'. Josh, though a
thorn in his flesh, sorts it all out for him.
[See colour section, page (b).]

The Red House Mystery

A.A. MILNE

Methuen 1922
artist: **Frank Wright**

A.A. Milne wrote only one detective
novel: *The Red House Mystery*. It was
extremely popular when first published and
still has an attraction for today's readers. A
man identified as Robert Ablett is shot
between the eyes in the study at the Red
House and discovered by Antony
Gillingham and Matthew Cayley. Antony
and his friend Bill Beverley act as a
Sherlock Holmes and Dr Watson team and
solve the murder. Frank Wright's design
shows the croquet box over the entrance to
a secret passage. Appearing 'so dramatically
out of the box' is 'that wonderful new kind
of croquet-ball': the head of Matthew
Cayley, who is raising the lid and looking
concerned. 'A shadow on the wall' appears
behind. [See colour section, page (b).]

The Case of the April Fools

CHRISTOPHER BUSH

Cassell 1933
artist: **unknown**

The Case of the April Fools begins with
threats to Charles Crewe that he will die
on 1 April, All Fools' Day. Ludovic
Travers is on hand when his corpse is duly
discovered on the appropriate morning.
His host, Courtney Allard, makes the
discovery, which features on the wrapper:
'Allard began to make queer little noises
and ... backed into the doorway'. The
artist has followed the text in depicting
him with a 'codfish face', 'eyes that bulged
... chin that receded and nose that
dominated the whole'. Allard himself is the
next victim, in decidedly short order:
Travers finds him dead on his return from
phoning the police. [See colour section,
page (b).]

Death in a Little Town

R.C. WOODTHORPE

Nicholson & Watson 1935
artist: **unknown**

Death in a Little Town is the first of two
novels by R.C. Woodthorpe with Matilda
Perks as detective. Miss Perks is 'like an
extremely ferocious edition of Queen
Victoria', an 'old vulture' with a harsh
voice and venomous tongue. She also has
'a passion for truth', shared by her
outspoken parrot, Ramsay MacDonald.
The death of the title is that of Douglas
Bonar, an unpopular landlord, seemingly at
odds with the entire local community. He
dies from 'a crack on the skull from a
spade' after an organized demonstration
against him. The wrapper shows Michael
Holt, the owner of the spade, getting it
back to his garden shed after removing it
from the vicinity of the body. [See colour
section, page (b).]

3
Scene of the Crime

The Cartwright Gardens Murder

J.S. FLETCHER

Collins 1924
artist: **Nick**

Nick's stylish design for J.S. Fletcher's *The Cartwright Gardens Murder*, in dark blue, black and grey, shows the elegant corpse of Alfred Jakyn, stretched out at the base of a street light in Cartwright Gardens, his hat and cane nearby. He has been 'a tallish, well-built man', who 'carried a cane, swinging it jauntily'. Jennison, a bored clerk longing for excitement, watches from his window and sees him suddenly 'cast the stick away from him, let out a strange, half-stifled cry, and, lifting both hands' begin 'tearing at his neckwear, as if he was being throttled'. Then he plunges 'straight forward on the pavement'.

A Fletcher mystery story, and a fine one.

The Sloane Square Mystery

HERBERT ADAMS

Methuen 1925
artist: **Frank Marston**

For Herbert Adams' *The Sloane Square Mystery* Frank Marston depicts the discovery of Sir Nicholas Brannock's body in Sloane Square, one Sunday at half-past one in the morning: 'Lying in the shadows, between the tall memorial and a low granite fountain some few feet from it, lay the prostrate figure of a man ... He was in evening dress and his hat lay a few feet away.' The two young men are The Honourable Edward Lamport, or 'Ned', and Bruce Graham, or 'Spider', the latter of whom recognizes the dead man as the uncle of his friend Rollo. He regards the death of Sir Nicholas as 'a slice of luck' for his friend, who has 'had a bad time lately' and is his uncle's heir: 'The old gentleman might have lived for another twenty years.'

A Mystery Story striking an entirely new note
for this master of fiction

The Grey Room

EDEN PHILLPOTTS

Hurst & Blackett 1921
artist: **Doco**

Eden Phillpotts, who also used the pseudonym 'Harrington Hext', wrote many crime novels, some, unfortunately, with unbelievable plots. *The Grey Room*, in which many people die, is at Chadlands, the home of the Lennox family. Doco's grey and pink design illustrates the room, which is 'large and commodious, with a rather fine oriel window'. 'Round the curve of the oriel ran a cushioned seat … Some old carved chairs stood round the walls, and in one corner, stacked together, lay half a dozen oil portraits … against the inner wall rose a single four poster bed of Spanish chestnut, also carved.' The skeletal arm stretching across the room hints at some deadly secret from the past.

The Long Good-bye

RAYMOND CHANDLER

Hamish Hamilton 1953
artist: **Fritz Wegner**

Raymond Chandler is one of America's finest detective writers. His celebrated private detective, Philip Marlowe, has an unforgettable line in wisecracks and always does his best for his clients, often endangering himself in the course of duty. In *The Long Good-bye*, he is hired by Terry Lennox but is unable to prevent the murder of Sylvia Lennox, found murdered shortly afterwards in their guest house. Fritz Wegner creates the murder scene as seen through an open doorway. The lights are on and a blue wrap has been thrown over a chair. Sylvia Lennox lies 'as naked as a mermaid on the bed'. Her face has been beaten 'to pieces with a bronze statuette of a monkey', which lies on the floor near her drooping arm.

The Silent Pool

PATRICIA WENTWORTH

Hodder & Stoughton 1956
artist: **unknown**

Patricia Wentworth's *The Silent Pool* is the 25th case for private detective Miss Maud Silver. 'Maudie', a former governess, is equipped with strong moral principles and a passion for justice. Adriana Ford consults Miss Silver when she suspects that someone is trying to murder her. Later, during a cocktail party at Ford House, a murder does occur, but the victim is the retired actress, Mabel Preston. The wrapper shows her in her coat 'with its great black and white checks', having 'passed into the flower garden … where there was a pool and seat'. She is 'startled' by a 'small bright light (that) came flickering through an arch in the hedge' but has 'no time to turn or cry out'.

The Case of the Running Man

CHRISTOPHER BUSH

Macdonald 1958
artist: **Blandford**

The Case of the Running Man takes Ludovic Travers to Joseph Borne's Kensington antiques shop. When another man enters Travers moves to talk to him, knowing him to be involved in his current investigation, though unaware of his name. He is foiled, however, by the proprietor, who hustles the man out of the shop and prevents Travers from following him, 'cleverly blocking' his way. Blandford's meticulous picture is both faithful and pleasing: Ludo looks as we have always known him and the others are precisely as described, the running man all in grey, Borne 'shortish', with 'hair so fair you could hardly discern where the grey began' and 'startling blue' eyes.

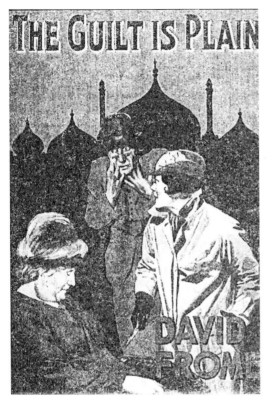

The Guilt is Plain

DAVID FROME

Longmans, Green 1938
artist: **unknown**

The Guilt is Plain is set in Brighton, where Mr Pinkerton is staying at Mrs Mortlake's 'dingy boarding-house'. In the Music Room at the Royal Pavilion, he comes upon the scene depicted, with great fidelity, on the wrapper. The 'domineering old woman' he has previously seen in a 'grey Rolls' now sits in her bath-chair, a 'shining red streak creeping ... down her large silken bosom'. Before her is the 'rigid raincoated figure' of the woman who has accused him of following her by the octopus tank at the Aquarium. Her face is 'transfigured by ... horror' and there is a 'small blood-stained paring knife in her black-gloved hand'.

Murder in Maryland

LESLIE FORD

Hutchinson n.d. (1933)
artist: **Harry Anderson**

Murder in Maryland is early Leslie Ford, pre-Primrose and Latham. It introduces Lt Joseph Kelly of the Baltimore police, who is 'much shrewder' than 'his general Sunday-suited, automobile-mechanic manner and appearance' would suggest. He has only two recorded cases, of which this is the first. Harry Anderson records the eerie moment when Dr Fisher finds Miss Nettie Wyndham lying in bed, 'horribly, offensively dead'. On the bed, also dead, is the 'horrible hairless little beast, obese and rheumy-eyed' so disliked in life by the doctor, who narrates the story. Daphne Lake is also present.

"I pushed the door open and stepped into Miss Nettie's bedroom. And I instinctively knew that someone else was there. Death was in the room, waiting for us to come. I turned my light on the great four poster bed. There was Miss Nettie ... horribly, offensively dead. Then I saw the terrible thing. On the other side of the old woman was the Mexican hairless bitch, her teeth bared, her rheumy eyes staring. She was dead, too. Then I noticed on a table beside the bed, an overturned glass."

The Problem of the Wire Cage

JOHN DICKSON CARR

Hamish Hamilton 1940
artist: **Lowen**

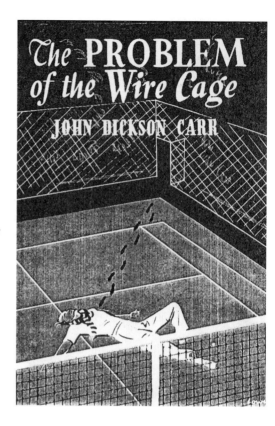

Lowen's design in green, brown and yellow perfectly captures the scene of the crime for *The Problem of the Wire Cage*: a tennis court, 'a brownish-grey rectangle, smooth as mud', doubly hemmed in by a 'darkish … enclosure of poplars' and 'its tall cage of wire'. The eleventh case for Dr Gideon Fell is another impossible crime from John Dickson Carr. Hugh Rowland and Brenda White discover Frank Dorrance, strangled on the tennis court, lying 'on his back not far from the middle of the court, his head towards the net'. 'Beginning at the little wire door, one set of footprints – Frank's – went straight out to the place where he lay.' No footprints have been left by his murderer.

The White Priory Murders

CARTER DICKSON

Heinemann 1935
artist: **unknown**

Carter Dickson's *The White Priory Murders* is the second case of Sir Henry Merrivale, who is staying at the White Priory when actress Marcia Tait is found with her 'head beaten in' in a pavilion in the garden known as the Queen's Mirror. Merrivale's nephew, James Bennett, arrives just as the body is discovered. The black and white wrapper shows the 'dull white' pavilion, standing 'in the middle of a snow-crusted clearing', with a line of freshly-made tracks leading to the front door. We see the 'figure [that] appeared in that doorway' and observe that 'no tracks came out'.

The Forty-first Passenger

KENNETH HOPKINS

Macdonald 1948
artist: **Stein**

The Forty-first Passenger is the second of
four novels with a newspaper reporter as
detective, alternating with Kenneth
Hopkins' other series, with Blow and
Manciple. Gerry Lee is a features writer on
The Daily Post and his current assignment
is to cover a coach tour of the West
Country, producing 'ten eight-hundred
word features … one a day by telephone
the night before'. The forty-first passenger
joins the coach en route and proves to
have 'escaped from Dartmoor less than
twenty-four hours earlier'. Stein's wrapper
shows the scene at Exeter, where Gerry
finds him 'on the back seat, in his usual
place' but knows 'at a glance he was dead'.

Let's Kill George

LUCY CORES

Cassell 1950
artist: **Arthur Barbosa**

Let's Kill George is the third of Lucy Cores'
four novels, an exuberant whodunit with a
celebrated screenwriter and dramatist as
victim. George Banat is 'found semi-
conscious at the foot of the stairs' in his
'remodelled' Connecticut farmhouse and
dies soon after 'without a word to
anybody'. Did he fall or was he pushed?
Since the treads are 'so small that one
practically had to go up sideways', the
former is possible; but a multiplicity of
motives suggests the latter. Barbosa shows
the 'satin smooth' banisters sweeping
'down in a lovely curve', with George
supine in the hall below.

The Blatchington Tangle

G.D.H. AND M. COLE

Collins 1926
artist: **E.P.**

The Blatchington Tangle is the second title
signed jointly by the Coles and features a
rare appearance by their detective, Henry
Wilson, as a private investigator. It also
introduces the Hon. Everard Blatchington,
who recurs in later novels as his amateur
second-string. Here the mystery involves
the Blatchington rubies and the dead
stranger found at Blatchington Towers the
morning after an attempt has been made to
steal them. E.P.'s brown wrapper shows
Dick Prescot kneeling beside the body,
having encountered it 'just inside the open
window' of the library on returning from
his morning bathe. The artist does not
show us the revolver tied to one of the
dead man's hands with 'a length of stout
green cord'.

Who murdered the mysterious
stranger at Blatchington Towers?

A COLLINS DETECTIVE NOVEL

He Found Himself Murdered

D.L. AMES

Swan 1947
artist: **unknown**

He Found Himself Murdered is from the
'D.L. Ames' phase of Delano Ames' career
and precedes the first of the Jane and
Dagobert novels by a year. It is a zestful
spy thriller in a more conventional mode
than the more sophisticated later work.
The wrapper records the scene that
launches the action, in which Steve
Brabazon undergoes 'an experience almost
unique: namely, being a spectator of his
own death'. The artist renders faithfully his
discovery of his own 'exact double',
'sprawled on his back' in Room 283 of the
Grand Hotel des Anglais in Ostend, 'the
handle of an ugly stiletto' protruding 'just
above his heart', his shirt 'soaked in
blood'.

Death on the Oxford Road

E.C.R. LORAC

Sampson Low 1933
artist: **Frank Sherwin**

Frank Sherwin's wrapper for E.C.R. Lorac's *Death on the Oxford Road* shows Chief-Inspector Robert Macdonald leaving his Talbot motor car at 1.15 in the morning on the Tetsworth to Wycombe road in Oxfordshire. He is concerned to ascertain whether the driver of 'the Sunbeam pulled up a few yards ahead' has knocked down the man 'lying prone across the road', the car 'in direct line with his body'. The man standing over the corpse is Dick Waring, chauffeur to Colonel Hanton's daughter, Diana. 'To the left, the road was bordered by a steep bank of chalk covered with a thick growth of dogwood and wayfaring tree.'

The End of Mr. Garment

VINCENT STARRETT

Doubleday Crime Club 1932
artist: **unknown (illegible)**

The End of Mr. Garment is the last of the three recorded cases of Walter Ghost, the dilettante polymath 'always in demand' as 'a sort of high-class trouble-shooter'. He investigates the murder of Stephen Garment, 'an eminent British novelist', murdered in a Chicago taxi, 'while a handful of guests await his coming in the handsome home of Mr. Howland Kimbark'. On arrival at the 'lake-front dwelling', the cab-driver, believing his passenger to be drunk, seeks 'help to carry him in'; but those who go to assist find themselves 'shocked and silent in the presence of the dead man, lying back against the cushions' of the cab. The black and yellow wrapper makes vivid the moment.

The Mysterious Affair at Styles

AGATHA CHRISTIE

Bodley Head 1921
artist: **Alfred James Dewey**

The Mysterious Affair at Styles was Agatha Christie's debut novel and the first case for Hercule Poirot and his Watson, Captain Arthur Hastings. The latter is invited by John Cavendish to stay at his family home, Styles Court, ruled by the matriarch, Mrs Inglethorpe. Twelve days later, he is awakened by Lawrence Cavendish, who takes him to his mother's locked bedroom, where 'the most alarming sounds were audible'. When they 'stumbled in together, Lawrence still holding his candle', they find Mrs Inglethorpe 'lying on the bed, her whole form agitated by violent convulsions'. After a 'final convulsion' she falls back 'motionless'. Dewey faithfully records the scene. [See colour section, page (c).]

Sky-rocket

MARY FITT

Nicholson & Watson 1938
artist: **unknown**

Sky-rocket is the novel in which Mary Fitt introduces Superintendent Mallett, the shrewd, imperturbable Scot who figures in most of her detective fiction. Here he investigates the murder of Nastasya Gromov during a fireworks party at Lakeside Grange. She has been a spiteful, sadistic 'hell-cat', disliked or feared by everyone else in the company. The artist shows considerable licence, depicting her in a red dress on the floor of the summerhouse; whereas the text has her in green, 'her fair head … fallen forward onto the table'. In the boat, the actor Reynold should be rowing, not reclining. [See colour section, page (c).]

The Case of the Constant Suicides

JOHN DICKSON CARR

Hamish Hamilton 1941
artist: **Hookway Cowles**

That great eccentric detective, Dr Gideon Fell, investigates in John Dickson Carr's *The Case of the Constant Suicides*. Several people have died by throwing themselves from the window of a tower at the Castle of Shira, depicted on Hookway Cowles' distinguished wrapper: 'Most of all you noticed the tower. Round, and of moss-patched grey stone, it reared up to a conical slate roof'. It appears 'to have only one window … set close up near the roof'. Alan Campbell stands anxiously by the body of the latest victim, lying 'face downwards on the flagstones': 'Colin Campbell – or a bundle of red-and-white striped pyjamas which might once have been Colin'. 'Sixty feet above his head the leaves of the window stood open.' [See colour section, page (c).]

The Body in the Silo

RONALD A. KNOX

Hodder & Stoughton n.d. (1933)
artist: **Bip Pares**

The Body in the Silo involves Miles and Angela Bredon in a nocturnal 'eloping party' at Lastbury Hall in Hereford. The participants career about the Malvern Hills in their cars at midnight. Next morning, the lion of the party is found in the Lastbury silo, dead from the 'carbonic acid gas' given off by the fermenting vegetation within. The silo figures prominently on Bip Pares' wrapper, 'a large building made like a lighthouse, forty feet high', with a 'gaunt cylindrical wall that towered up' to a 'conical top' and a pulley for hoisting up the bundles of vegetable matter 'ripe for immurement'. [See colour section, page (c).]

End of an Ancient Mariner

G.D.H. AND M. COLE

Collins Crime Club 1933
artist: **Youngman Carter**

End of an Ancient Mariner is a domestic tangle with its roots in the past and Superintendent Wilson as detective. The eponymous sailor is Captain John Jay, who meets his end reeking of rum at the Hampstead home of Philip Blakeway, with whom he has a score to settle. Youngman Carter shows him lying dead on his back, with a revolver in his hand. Philip Blakeway stands over him and Major Sayers kneels beside him. Lying 'open face downwards on the floor not far from the body' is the book on golf that Blakeway has 'flung … at him', supposedly in the belief that he has surprised a burglar. [See colour section, page (d).]

Inspector French and the Cheyne Mystery

FREEMAN WILLS CROFTS

Collins 1926
artist: **C. Morse**

Freeman Wills Crofts' *Inspector French and the Cheyne Mystery* is the second investigation for Joseph French. Maxwell Cheyne, country gentleman and author, has his pockets searched after being drugged at the Edgecombe Hotel in Plymouth. Subsequently, his home is burgled and he is kidnapped; and when he escapes, he is attacked and knocked unconscious. Morse shows Joan Merrill's discovery of Cheyne after he has 'gradually struggled back to consciousness' and 'after superhuman efforts … succeeded in reaching the paling separating the lot from Hopefield Avenue'. He has 'sunk down exhausted' and lain 'for some time … motionless in a state of coma'. Inspector French sits thoughtfully by a telephone. [See colour section, page (d).]

4
Deadly Demesnes

The Six Queer Things

C. ST JOHN SPRIGG

Herbert Jenkins 1937
artist: **Alex Jardine**

The Six Queer Things is the last of C. St
John Sprigg's novels, published after his
death in the Spanish Civil War. It must
have appealed instantly to its publisher,
who made something of a speciality of
lurid, hectic thrillers. When Marjorie
Easton enters the service of Michael
Crispin and his sister she puts her sanity at
risk: the object of most of the characters is
to drive her mad. After sinister events in
London, she is 'kidnapped … and forcibly
imprisoned' in a 'mental home', an
'abominable place' built 'on a slightly
rising ground' in a desolate landscape.
Jardine's black and green wrapper
admirably conveys 'the strangeness of the
scene and its deserted, mournful aspect'.

The Shadow on the Downs

R.C. WOODTHORPE

Nicholson & Watson 1935
artist: **Sparrow**

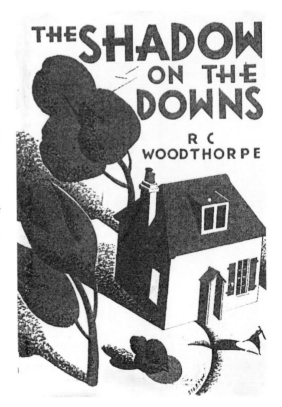

The Shadow on the Downs marks the second
appearance of Miss Matilda Perks, self-
defined as 'an evil old woman'. On a visit
to her nephew, she arrives in time for the
murder of an odious councillor, found
dead in the church porch. A second corpse
is discovered by Mrs Charteris driven
'within the walls of Rosemary Cottage' by
a thunderstorm. Sparrow's wrapper shows
her reaction to the sight of 'the body of
Mrs. Burwash, lying in a crumpled heap
on the floor … her face contorted by the
agony of a frightful death'. She runs out
'into the full force of the storm', the
lightning playing round her 'as she fled
like a mad thing down the lane', uttering
'cries of utter despair'.

Poison in Jest

JOHN DICKSON CARR

Hamish Hamilton 1932
artist: **V. Asta**

Poison in Jest is one of John Dickson Carr's
most atmospheric novels. The menace and
evil show strongly in Asta's blue, black and
white wrapper, depicting a nocturnal view
of the open gates of Judge Quayle's house,
with the house beyond. 'The iron gates of
the Quayle house sagged open. The house
was as huge and grotesque as ever', its
towers 'black monstrosities against
starlight'; but 'it needed paint', its lawns
are 'unkempt' and 'there was an
atmosphere of dinginess about it'. Jeff
Marle, returning to the house after many
years, is present when Judge Quayle is
poisoned. He and Pat Rossiter share an
investigation notable for unrelieved tension
and fear.

The House of Cain

ARTHUR W. UPFIELD

Hutchinson 1928
artist: **unknown**

Arthur Upfield's first novel, *The House of
Cain*, is aptly named, since the isolated
edifice in question was created by a triple
murderer as an establishment for fellow
killers: 'Of necessity the Home must be at
a safe distance from civilisation … Here in
this vast semi-desert … we found what I
wanted.' The wrapper, in black, orange
and yellow, shows the grim, tower-like
house built on barren rock. Martin
Sherwood, editor-in-chief of the *Melbourne
Daily Tribune*, becomes swept up in an
exciting adventure arising from the
occupants of 'The House of Cain'. His
fiancee, Austiline Thorpe, and his fearless
brother Monty are also involved.

*The breathless tale of a murder settlement in the heart of the
Australian Bush*

A Louse for the Hangman

LEO BRUCE

Peter Davies 1958
artist: **Biro**

Under the pseudonym of Leo Bruce,
Rupert Croft-Cooke wrote 31 detective
novels, all in the classic form. Carolus
Deene, a public schoolmaster with a
substantial private income, is one of his
two series detectives. In *A Louse for the
Hangman* he investigates the murders of
two men at Highcastle Manor. Biro's
effective design for the wrapper is
dominated by a hanging noose, brown
against a dark grey and blue sky. Beneath is
the neo-classical manor, set among trees
and lawns: 'the work of Vanbrugh, a
smaller but no less perfectly proportioned
Blenheim'. 'The house was quite perfect,
not a brick or a mullion out of keeping …
It even had the two-storey columns in a
similarly imposing entrance.'

Death and the Shortest Day

MARY FITT

Macdonald 1952
artist: **Broom Lynne**

Death and the Shortest Day opens with the
marriage of John Scoon and Eva Paull,
both of whom have lost their previous
spouses. The bride is immediately
widowed for the second time, when her
new husband is found dead on the
wedding-night, with a pistol on the rug
beside him. Superintendent Mallett
investigates, with Dr Fitzbrown in
attendance. Broom Lynne's wrapper is
appropriately sombre, with Scoon Hall
snowbound among winter trees: an
'enormous house', 'long and low', 'built in
the 1930s when building was at its
cheapest'. Exploding overhead is the
rocket that so complicates Mallett's
investigation.

Something Nasty in the Woodshed

ANTHONY GILBERT

Collins Crime Club 1942
artist: **Thompson**

Anthony Gilbert's *Something Nasty in the Woodshed* has a black, blue and cream wrapper with a strongly atmospheric composition by Thompson. When Edmund Durward takes the tenancy of The Haven, he remarks: 'I'm going to find that woodshed useful.' Later, when Arthur Crook sees Durward's advertisement 'to meet a Gentlewoman of Independent means', he asks Bill Parsons to file it as 'There may be a job of work for us within the year'. Durward marries Agatha Forbes but spends many hours working in the woodshed. When she investigates the shed one evening, she finds 'It was larger than she had realised and contained … a number of trunks, boxes and packing cases'; when she leaves it she is 'so shaken and aghast that she was scarcely sane'.

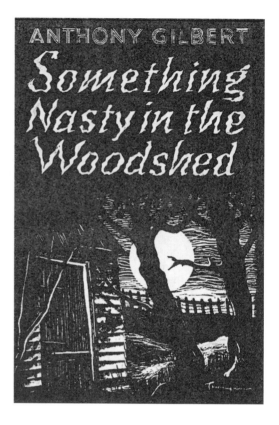

Death of an Aryan

ELSPETH HUXLEY

Methuen 1939
artist: **C.W. Bacon**

Death of an Aryan is the third and last of Elspeth Huxley's Superintendent Vachell novels, all set in East Africa, where she lived for some years. The victim is Karl Munson, a German settler with Nazi sympathies and a reputation for brutality. He dies in the 'pyrethrum-drying shed' on his farm, shown on C.W. Bacon's black and blue wrapper among other farm buildings, although the text puts it 'a little distance beyond' them. It is a 'two-storey building made of cut stone, taller than it was long or broad' and 'perched up like a square church steeple without the church'. The corrugated iron roof has 'long slits on each side of the ridge-beam' for ventilation.

A CRIME CONNOISSEUR BOOK
MURDER AT LANDRED HALL
JAMES TURNER

Murder at Landred Hall

JAMES TURNER

Cassell 1954
artist: **Edward Pagram**

Murder at Landred Hall is the first of James Turner's distinctive mystery novels, all with antiquarian Rampion Savage as detective. His arrival in freezing weather at Landred in Suffolk coincides with the murder of John Summers, the bailiff for the estate, and the disappearance of a reliquary containing a thorn from the Crown of Thorns. Pagram shows the 'ruined mansion' enveloped by 'the stillness of the frozen world'. It rises 'like the massif of a mountain', 'immense and impossibly huge' and rendering Rampion 'speechless' by its 'beauty'. Its partial ruination dates from the war, when it was 'hit by a stray stick of bombs from a fleeing German 'plane'.

The Mortover Grange Mystery

J.S. FLETCHER

Herbert Jenkins 1926
artist: **Philip Simmonds**

Philip Simmonds has created a starkly effective design for J.S. Fletcher's *The Mortover Grange Mystery*. In the foreground, an arm is exposed in a snowdrift, while the Grange appears purple against a threatening night sky, framed by bare, black trees. The house is 'cut off from the world', its 'timbered walls, quaint chimneys and whitewashed gables' making 'a picture against the dark hillside'. To Detective-Sergeant Wedgwood, arriving to deal with a fascinating case involving several deaths, it is an 'eerie place' with 'an air of gloom and silence' about it.

THE
MORTOVER
GRANGE
MYSTERY
J.S. FLETCHER

The elucidation of the mystery makes absorbing reading. The author knows how to hold his readers' attention up to the last page.

FOR SUMMARY OF THIS STORY SEE BACK OF WRAPPER

The House in Lordship Lane

A.E.W. MASON

Hodder & Stoughton 1946
artist: **Leslie Stead**

The House in Lordship Lane is the last of the
Hanaud–Ricardo novels of A.E.W. Mason.
Daniel Horbury was one of 'two rogues
who cheated a Parisian years ago' and has
since become MP for Kempston and an
'obese Romeo' twice the age of his Juliet.
Hanaud and Mr Ricardo are summoned to
White Barn, the 'small manor house' in
south London where Horbury is found
with his throat cut. Stead shows the house
with its 'screen of holly' and the lit
window of the Horburys' bedroom. It is 'a
pleasant oblong unpretentious house … of
two storeys only' with the door 'in the
centre, with a large window on either
side'. Outside, incongruously, is a bus stop.

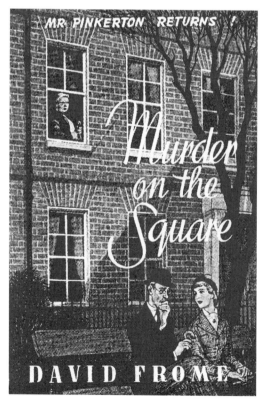

Murder on the Square

DAVID FROME

Hale n.d. (1951)
artist: **? Sax**

Murder on the Square marks the return of
Mr Pinkerton after a protracted absence.
He now lives at 4 Godolphin Square in
London, a house with sinister secrets,
where Arthur Pegott is murdered and he
himself is 'conked on the bean'. Up on the
first floor Miss Caroline Winship sits all
day 'brooding over the ruins of her
bombed-out house across the Square'.
Outside is the 'dilapidated bench' on
which Mr Pinkerton likes to sit, 'out of
the range of Miss Myrtle Grimstead's
managerial eye'. On the wrapper, which is
surely by Sax, Mary Winship sits beside
him. She, at least, he knows he can trust.

To Let. Furnished.

JOSEPHINE BELL

Methuen 1952
artist: **Oliver Carson**

To Let. Furnished. is an absorbing suspense novel set in and around the temporary home of a diplomat's wife, neurotic about her emotional past. Once established at Wentforth Grange in Dorset, she begins to assemble the history of the house and its owners, with devastating consequences for herself. Oliver Carson's blue wrapper shows the 'elegant exterior' of the Grange: 'The wide door, with fanlight and overhanging porch, was flanked on either side by a row of windows long and wide, with low sills a couple of feet from the ground. Their beautiful proportions were matched by a similar row of smaller windows above.'

The Woman at Belguardo

MARGARET ERSKINE

Hodder & Stoughton 1961
artist: **Leslie Wood**

The Woman at Belguardo was Lisa Harcourt, who has played the *femme fatale* once too often and now lies dead in her garden-room, her beauty obliterated. Her house is shown by Leslie Wood, who follows carefully Margaret Erskine's text. Set among hills, 'steep and heavily wooded, with tall fir trees', it has white walls, a 'long double row of windows' and 'a surprising and frivolous-looking dome'. 'Urns decorated the flat roof' and 'Six narrow steps led to a door of carved Italian walnut'. Dr Mark Warry stands before the house with P.C. Peters. Septimus Finch has not yet arrived. The dominant colour is red, for the sky, the hills and the drive.

And Then There Were None

AGATHA CHRISTIE

Dodd, Mead 1940
artist: **unknown**

And Then There Were None has probably
the cleverest plot in the history of crime
fiction and represents Agatha Christie's
finest hour. The wrapper shows Fred
Narracott's boat approaching Indian Island.
It will bring the ten people invited to the
lonely mansion on the island, 'low and
square and modern looking' and 'facing
south'. The guests have 'their first glimpse
of Indian Island' by the light of 'the setting
sun': 'There was something sinister about'
the 'boldly silhouetted rock with its faint
resemblance to a giant Indian's head'. The
skeletal hand hints at the deaths to come –
the 'ten dead bodies and … unsolved
problem' awaiting the men who eventually
come from the mainland.

The Crime in the Dutch Garden

HERBERT ADAMS

Methuen 1931
artist: **Guy Fry**

Guy Fry's strikingly modernistic design for
Herbert Adams' *The Crime in the Dutch
Garden* is green, mauve, black and white.
It depicts Merrow Craig with part of its
extensive gardens: a 'French garden, a
miniature Versailles, with pools and
splashing fountains', 'an old English garden
with roses' and the Dutch garden where
Miss Annabelle Querdling is killed when a
garden ornament is pushed onto her:
'There was a second chair. One arm was
broken and stains of blood marred its
white paint. Beside it was the base of the
figure.' Barrister Jimmie Haswell assists the
police in their investigation but a further
murder occurs before he unravels the plot
and reveals the truth.

Octagon House

PHOEBE ATWOOD TAYLOR

Collins Crime Club 1938
artist: **Alex Jardine**

Octagon House is 'the old eight sided
Sparrow place', familiar from boyhood to
Asey Mayo, who has family links with the
Sparrows. He is driven to turning up to
putty its windows in order to be on the
spot after Pamela Frye's obnoxious sister is
murdered and a 'huge lump' of ambergris,
worth a fortune, disappears. He gets into
the house at cellar level, discovering 'two
triangular small rooms, two rectangles …
and two hybrid rooms that seemed to have
at least six walls apiece'. The hall runs
'diagonally through the place … slicing the
octagon' and a circular staircase links the
floors. The wheelbarrow on Jardine's
wrapper contains the ambergris.

Disappearance of Dr. Bruderstein

JOHN SHERWOOD

Hodder & Stoughton n.d. (1949)
artist: **Bip Pares**

Disappearance of Dr. Bruderstein is the first of
John Sherwood's novels and launches the
career of the Treasury trouble-shooter
Charles Blessington, here a member of the
Control Commission in Berlin in August
1945. Having witnessed the abduction of
Dr Karl von Bruderstein, he feels impelled
to investigate, in the hope of effecting a
rescue. His inquiries take him to the
Schloss Lippenheim near Kassel, 'built on a
small, bare spur that stood out from the
hillsides'. With its 'grey walls, overhanging
a sheer drop' and a 'squat pepperpot
tower' it is 'certainly a romantic sight'.
The jeep 'Alice' occupies the foreground,
with Driver Parsons at the wheel and Mr
Blessington upright beside him.

The White Cottage Mystery

MARGERY ALLINGHAM

Jarrolds n.d. (1928)
artist: **P. Youngman Carter**

The White Cottage Mystery is the first of Margery Allingham's crime novels, ante-dating the arrival of Albert Campion. Youngman Carter's wrapper shows Eric Crowther's approach to the White Cottage, 'coming across the lawn with the gun under his arm ... as if he'd just come in from the woods'. He looks, properly, 'a most unpleasant person', which is what the detective, W.T. Challoner, calls him. Soon after, he is shot by the least likely person present. The White Cottage appears L-shaped, with red roofs overhung by huge trees. Estah Phillips is watching from a balcony, but neither she nor it is shown. [See colour section, page (d).]

Case in the Clinic

E.C.R. LORAC

Collins Crime Club 1941
artist: **Stead**

For E.C.R. Lorac's *Case in the Clinic*, Stead has drawn the entrance to the grounds of White Gables in green and black on white. He shows the 'tall gate-posts and wrought iron gate which gave on to the drive' and, beyond, the 'beautifully-kept lawns towards the dignified house'. Lee Gordon is the tenant of White Gables, where the Reverend Mr Anderby enjoys helping in the garden and greenhouse. When Major Grendon witnesses Anderby's death in the garden, he is very suspicious of the circumstances, especially since the vicar's new wife, an ex-nurse, has inherited several legacies from deceased former patients. Major Grendon's own death – by gas, at Max Brook's clinic – leads to an investigation by Chief-Inspector Robert Macdonald of Scotland Yard. [See colour section, page (d).]

5
The Watchers

The Fatal Five Minutes

R.A.J. WALLING

Hodder & Stoughton 1932
artist: **Leslie Stead**

The Fatal Five Minutes introduces Philip Tolefree, R.A.J. Walling's major series detective, ostensibly an insurance agent but actually a specialist in 'the kind of thing City men wanted', 'financial inquiries' discreetly conducted. A routine assignment involves him for the first time in a murder investigation, when his employer, Wellington Burnet, is clubbed to death with a candlestick at his country home. Tolefree's Watson is Mr Farrar, a City friend, depicted by Stead on the second landing at the London chambers of Edward Cossor, KC in The Temple, where he 'could lean over the banisters and watch and listen'. Below an angry woman unknown to him departs in dudgeon, moving with 'quick steps down the stone stairs'.

Danger Calling

PATRICIA WENTWORTH

Hodder & Stoughton 1931
artist: **unknown**

The stylish wrapper for Patricia Wentworth's *Danger Calling* has a pale background tinged with green. Lindsay Trevor, in black coat and hat, stands at the corner of Leaham Road with Elsie Manning, in a red outfit trimmed with white. Trevor peers through the fog to check that they are not being followed, while Elsie ensures that no one is lurking in the shop. The two have been thrown together by wholly unexpected circumstances including the element of blackmail. Elsie has the key to the 'dark empty shop with a fog right up to the windows' and they enter together, despite the fact that she does not know she can trust him.

Up the Garden Path

MILES BURTON

Collins Crime Club 1941
artist: **Leslie Stead**

The butler of Valley View, a large mansion in the village of Downspring, is found murdered on the garden path of the village policeman. Inspector Arnold of the CID at Scotland Yard arrives on the scene and murder again occurs. Desmond Merrion, now working for Admiralty Intelligence, is also in the area investigating suspected spies. Stead's wrapper for Miles Burton's *Up the Garden Path* has a green, black and white design picturing the police closing in on Valley View. Merrion raises himself 'cautiously to his knees … he could see the dark figures of his two companions'. The officers carry weapons because it is certain that the members of the gang, when cornered, 'will fight for their lives'.

They Watched by Night

JOHN RHODE

Collins Crime Club 1941
artist: **Thompson**

They Watched by Night is a wartime case for Dr Priestley, with Superintendent Hanslet and Jimmy Waghorn, the former metamorphosed into 'Mr. Farland of Chestnut Cottage, Hoxdown', the latter 'on a confidential mission', having been 'lent by the Yard to Military Intelligence for the duration'. Their joint concern is a leakage of information to the enemy, resulting in repeated bombings of a top secret research camp. Thompson shows Jimmy in his 'heavy overcoat' at the 'observation post' covering the eastern side of the terrain. The crescent moon is there by artistic licence: the text demands a 'clear, moonless and very dark' night.

Uncommon Cold

E.H. CLEMENTS

Hodder & Stoughton 1958
artist: **George Chrichard**

Uncommon Cold opens with the scene depicted by George Chrichard on its wrapper, on the promenade at Scrimborough, a 'bleak, unlovely and inaccessible' seaside town in the off-season. Two of the three men shown are professional watchers: Alister Woodhead, looking out to sea to the left of the shelter, and the young Russian in the foreground, whose brief is to keep the third man under constant observation, lest he defect to the West. The object of their joint interest is Vladimir Remin, a delegate at an international conference organized in Scrimborough by the Ministry for Scientific Research. He is the shadowy figure on the right.

New Graves at Great Norne

HENRY WADE

Constable 1947
artist: **unknown**

Henry Wade's *New Graves at Great Norne* is a classic whodunit set in a small east coast market town. Great Norne is first disturbed by the death of the Reverend Theobald Torridge, its vicar. Other deaths occur and Scotland Yard is brought in to help track down the murderer. The wrapper pictures Mr Torridge standing at 'the gate leading from his garden to the churchyard' and looking lovingly at his church, St Martha's in its setting: 'The moon was shining now upon a far corner of the churchyard, illuminating a small white cross that stood by itself, close up against the dark yews.' As he watches, a shadow moves, revealing itself 'as a dark figure, with the glimmer of a white face'.

The Hammersmith Murders

DAVID FROME

Methuen 1930
artist: **E.P.K.**

The Hammersmith Murders introduces
Inspector J. Humphrey Bull and his
landlord in Golders Green, Mr Pinkerton
(here 'David', not 'Evan'). Bull is 'the
epitome of middle-class morality' and, so,
is particularly well-suited to murders in the
London suburbs. When Lawrence Sprague
dies in Hammersmith, the case is assigned
to him. The wrapper shows him peeping
through the parlour blind at 60, Caithness
Road: 'He put his eye to the slit and
found that he had a fair sight of the ...
room.' Eric Cutler is seen with upraised
arm, having just had a jug broken over his
head by his cousin, Beatrice Sprague.

Something about Midnight

D.B. OLSEN

Doubleday Crime Club 1950
artist: **Beecher**

Something about Midnight features Professor
Pennyfeather, who alternated for some
years with D.B. Olsen's better-known
detective, the resourceful spinster, Rachel
Murdock. He is persuaded to look into the
disappearance of Ernestine Hollister, one
of his students. The scene on the wrapper
is described in a letter from Freddy Nixon,
who has been involved with Ernestine.
Outside a mountain cabin beyond Los
Angeles, he watches and listens as she talks
to someone unseen with a 'horrible, happy
cruelty in her tone'. Beecher records
faithfully 'the fine fluff of her hair ... the
way she held a cigarette' and her scornful
demeanour. Only the billowing curtains
belie the text.

The Case of the Fighting Soldier

CHRISTOPHER BUSH

Cassell 1942
artist: **Jack Matthew**

The Case of the Fighting Soldier is set in No. 5 School for Instructors of Home Guard at Peakridge in Derbyshire, where Major Ludovic Travers is the second-in-command and Captain Mortar is something of a problem. A self-styled 'fighting soldier', openly contemptuous of those without front-line experience, he drinks too much and makes enemies easily. An 'accident' with a Mills bomb fails to put paid to him, but both he and his hut are finally 'blown … to smithereens' by a truly 'terrific explosion'. Jack Matthew shows him at his desk, while his killer watches through the open window.

Midnight Wireless

C.A. ALINGTON

Macdonald 1947
artist: **Crispin**

Midnight Wireless is post-war Alington, a light-hearted spy story with an elaborate editorial commentary as accompaniment to the narrative proper. Mr Templeton, the headmaster of Harchester School, has been 'seconded for military service' but appears to have died in the cause. The action is launched with the announcement of his death on a late-night news bulletin and Crispin records the moment when 'the silence was suddenly broken by the voice of the BBC announcer'. He also shows the 'three masked men' who have been watching Mr Templeton's cottage, prior to entering in search of a document essential to their continued wellbeing.

Walk with Care

PATRICIA WENTWORTH

Cassell 1933
artist: **Lance Cattermole**

Lance Cattermole's design for Patricia Wentworth's *Walk with Care* is black, touched with green, white and red. It shows a mysterious light emanating from a crystal ball, suffusing the features of Asphodel, who is staring intently as she cups it in her hands. The fortune teller's hair, lips and long finger nails are blood red. 'The hands that held the crystal were fallen into the shadows of her velvet draperies'. Silhouetted against the black and white background is Rosalind Denny, in a pill-box hat. She is watching the proceedings with intense interest: 'The shadows shook before her eyes. Gilbert's voice came from the lips in the pale tilted oval that was Asphodel's face.'

The Owl

JONATHAN GRAY

Harrap 1937
artist: **Jack Matthew**

Jonathan Gray was the pseudonym used by Herbert Adams for two of his crime novels. *The Owl* was written for Harrap's £1500 Cracksman Competition. Detective-Inspector Ashdown of Scotland Yard is investigating a series of jewel robberies causing consternation among London's smart set. He becomes convinced that the criminal, known as 'The Owl', is one of the four friends with whom he habitually plays golf. Jack Matthew's elegant nocturnal scene depicts The Owl in top hat and evening dress. He is watching to ensure that the coast is clear before entering Railton Priory in search of the Wheeler rubies, 'a prize worthy of his efforts'.

The Strong Room

R.A.J. WALLING

Jarrolds n.d. (1927)
artist: **unknown**

The Strong Room is the first of R.A.J.
Walling's novels and combines sober
detection with the carefree verve of the
thriller. Noel Pinson, a barrister, is
persuaded to inquire into the
disappearance of Westmore Colebroke
from his home in Longbridge, where a
corpse is discovered in a secret strong-
room hidden behind the panelling. The
quest takes him to Paris, where he finds
himself under observation from a
'gentleman of inconspicuous appearance,
in a lounge suit and a felt hat', who 'took
the same interest in his doings and paid the
same attention to his footsteps' whatever
his circumstances. The wrapper shows him
entering the Brasserie Boucher in the
Passage Michel, with 'Felt Hat' on the
alert round the next corner. [See colour
section, page (e).]

Sinners Go Secretly

ANTHONY WYNNE

Hutchinson n.d. (1927)
artist: **Nick**

Sinners Go Secretly is a unique collection of
stories featuring Eustace Hailey, the Harley
Street doctor who figures otherwise only
in novels by Anthony Wynne. Nick's
stylish period wrapper illustrates the first of
the 12 stories, 'The House in the Woods',
about a supposed adulteress. It shows the
scène à faire between Elsa Maltman and Sir
John Oldshaw, who stands before her
'with wild eyes and flaming cheeks', as if
to confirm the worst fears of Elsa's
husband, lurking outside the window, with
a pistol in his hand and Dr Hailey in
support. In the event, neither proves
necessary, since Elsa Maltman already has
the situation well in hand. [See colour
section, page (e).]

6
The Killers

A Savant's Vendetta

R. AUSTIN FREEMAN

Pearson 1920
artist: **A. Crick**

A Savant's Vendetta is an oddity among the
works of R. Austin Freeman in that it
failed to find a British publisher until six
years after its publication in America (as
The Uttermost Farthing). It features
Humphrey Challoner, the 'great savant'
who also appears in an uncollected story,
'The Mystery of Hoo Marsh'. Crick shows
him among the scientific apparatus of his
laboratory with, beside him, a vision of his
dead wife, Kate, as if remembering their
'unbroken concord, with mutual love that
grew from day to day'. The narrative gives
a gruesome account of his terrible revenge
on her murderer as, 'crazed, demented by
grief and horror', he discharges the 'debt
[that] had to be paid'.

The Brooklyn Murders

G.D.H. COLE

Collins 1923
artist: **Percy Graves**

The Brooklyn Murders is the first of the
Henry Wilson novels, signed by G.D.H.
Cole alone but later attributed also to his
wife, Margaret, subsequently his
acknowledged collaborator. The action
begins with double murder: of John
Prinsep, killed by a blow to the head and
stabbed to the heart after death; and of
George Brooklyn, struck by 'a savage
blow' from the club of a stone Hercules.
Joan Cowper is engaged to Prinsep but is
drawn to Robert Ellery, whose prompt
action saves her when the killer attempts
to add her to his victims: 'Ellery was just
too quick for him, knocking up his arm so
that the bullet embedded itself in the
ceiling.' Percy Graves admirably fixes the
moment.

The Venner Crime

JOHN RHODE

Odhams n.d. (1933)
artist: **V. Asta**

The Venner Crime is unique in the annals of Westbourne Terrace in that it culminates in a life-or-death 'duel' between Dr Priestley and the murderer of Ernest Venner, each of whom drinks a glass of liquid, one containing poison, the other bicarbonate of soda. Venner has been under suspicion of having murdered his uncle and his disappearance gives rise to further inquiries. Asta's wrapper shows Denis Hinchliffe's bedroom at 7 Clewer Street, with Hinchliffe's murderer reaching for the glass at his victim's bedside, having 'screwed himself up to the point of adding the Vermin Killer to that infernal medicine which Hinchliffe had prescribed for himself'.

The Waxworks Murder

JOHN DICKSON CARR

Hamish Hamilton 1932
artist: **V. Asta**

Journalist Jeff Marle is the narrator of John Dickson Carr's *The Waxworks Murder*. He describes the detection by the flamboyant Frenchman, Henri Bencolin, an adviser to the courts and Director of the Paris Police, here investigating the murders of two stabbed women. Claudine Martel's body is found inside the oldest waxworks in Paris, in the arms of the satyr, a 'man with humped shoulders, his face shaded by a mediaeval hood, but with a long jaw which carried a suggestion of a smile'. Asta shows the killer stalking the waxworks, his evil green face depicted on a black background: a 'green-lit ghost' with 'a heavy jaw', 'eyes which looked fixedly' and 'a knife in its hand'.

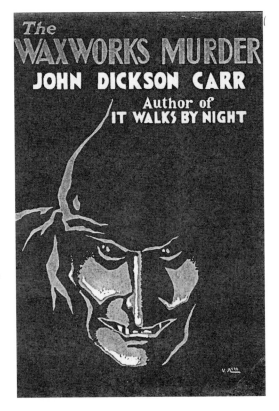

Death in a Duffle Coat

MILES BURTON

Collins Crime Club 1956
artist: **William Randell**

Death in a Duffle Coat is mature Burton, a complicated story, well-knit and continually teasing. Three people are murdered at the Lodge Cottage of Springlease Hall: one of its tenants, an inquisitive Canadian visitor and a popular low comedian. Even Desmond Merrion is hard put to it to establish the links among them and their murderer, shown by Randell appropriately clad, wielding the dagger used to kill the Canadian. The ubiquitous duffle-coat of the 1950s is an added complication; as Merrion ruefully reflects: 'the hood of a duffle-coat hid most of the head. Seen from the rear, it would be impossible to tell whether the wearer … was a man or a woman'.

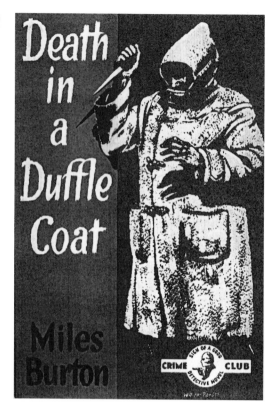

Plain Murder

C.S. FORESTER

Bodley Head 1930
artist: **S.G. Hulme Beaman**

C.S. Forester wrote two crime novels in addition to his celebrated Hornblower books. In *Plain Murder*, three clerks in an advertising agency resort to murder to prevent it becoming known that they have taken bribes from a competitor. Their problems are compounded when one of the three finds he cannot live with his crime and so has also to die. S.G. Hulme Beaman's design – in orange, black and purple on white – shows the two surviving conspirators caught in a web of mutual suspicion: 'Oldroyd, with his heavy face wrinkled with perplexity … sat at his table toiling over lay-outs … Behind him sat Morris … with his scowling brow, his woolly hair horrid with grease … and those wild-beast eyes.'

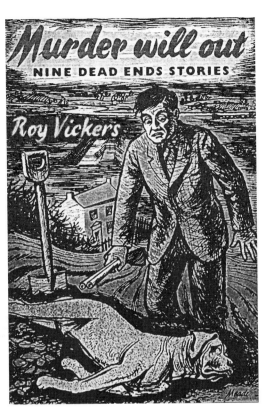

Murder Will Out

ROY VICKERS

Faber 1950
artist: **Meade**

Roy Vickers is justly famous for his Department of Dead Ends stories, which start by showing how and why the murder is committed and then describe how and why the murderer is caught. *Murder Will Out* contains nine of these stories: 'Kill me, Kill my Dog' is featured on the wrapper. Dennis Stretton loses his fiancée, Leonie, to Arthur Crouch, who also spoils his prospects of more lucrative employment. After Leonie's death, Crouch visits Stretton, accompanied by his dog, a mastiff. During an argument, Stretton grips Crouch by the throat and finds he has 'not choked [him] but broken his neck'. Meade shows Stretton burying the shot mastiff near its master, in his cottage garden on the Essex marshes. Six months later, Detective-Inspector Rason arrives, acting on 'a tip from that mastiff'.

The List of Adrian Messenger

PHILIP MACDONALD

Herbert Jenkins 1960
artist: **Coles**

The List of Adrian Messenger names ten men who prove to be the victims of murder made to look like accident. Coles' dramatic wrapper for this complex Philip MacDonald novel is partly framed by the names on the list. Gwendolynne LaDoll, an innocent typist, also has to die – and Anthony Gethryn is too late to save her: 'the lady met with an accident. In the Fulham Road ... She seems to have slipped off the kerb in front of a bus.' Gethryn and Superintendent Arnold Pike try to discover the connection linking the deaths and to find the ruthless killer: 'A man of middle-size ... with overcoat collar turned up and hat-brim turned down' and 'a little muscle at the corner of his right eye' given to 'involuntary twitching'.

X Esquire
LESLIE CHARTERIS

Ward, Lock 1927
artist: **Frank Marston**

Frank Marston's strikingly elegant wrapper
for Leslie Charteris' first book, *X Esquire*,
shows the moment after the door of Mr
Strange's study has 'swung wide
soundlessly' and 'X Esquire' has entered:
'The figure that stood on the threshold …
was a tall, broad-shouldered man in
evening dress. An Inverness cape hung
from his shoulders and in one hand he
held an opera hat. And over his head was a
black hood, the ends of which were
tucked into his collar.' Strange knows who
it is who has come for him and sees the
'face of iron' beneath the cowl before his
back is broken 'across the chair, as one
breaks a rotten stick'.

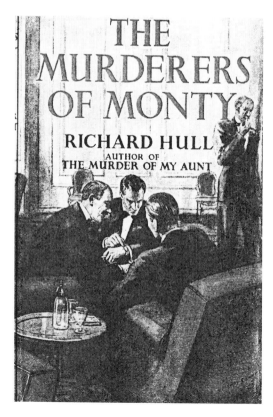

The Murderers of Monty
RICHARD HULL

Faber 1937
artist: **Hookway Cowles**

Richard Hull's 15 crime novels include
several of the inverted type. Hookway
Cowles shows the smoking room at the Pall
Mall Club on his very detailed wrapper for
The Murderers of Monty. Four members are
shown: P.R. ('Prunes') Unwin-Shackleton,
Arthur Bethel, John Kernside and Norman
Wrangham. Together they plot an elaborate
hoax whereby they will 'murder' Monty
Archer, about whom they 'are all agreed …
something has got to be done'. They 'form
a company for the purpose of doing so: to
be called the Murderers of Monty Limited'.
The first shareholder will poison him, the
second stab him, the third shoot him and
the fourth administer comfort. Monty,
however, is actually murdered: and things
look grim for the members of the company.

7
The Victims

Why Didn't They Ask Evans?

AGATHA CHRISTIE

Collins Crime Club 1934
artist: **Gilbert Cousland**

While Bobby Jones and Dr Thomas are playing golf at Marchbolt in Wales, Bobby mishits on the 17th tee and his ball goes over the cliff. On looking for the ball, he notices a body lying on the rocks below. Gilbert Cousland depicts Alan Carstairs, whom they discover dying of a broken back. He is a 'fine, healthy-looking fellow' and even the 'pallor of approaching death couldn't disguise the deep tan of the skin'. The artist records 'the white teeth showing through the parted lips' and the blue eyes, which 'suddenly opened'. Carstairs speaks in a clear voice: *Why Didn't They Ask Evans?* Then he shudders and dies. Agatha Christie's ingenious and exciting plot has Bobby searching for Evans and the murderer of Carstairs.

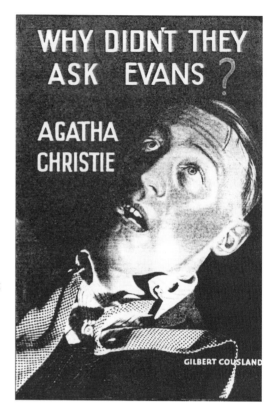

Lord Edgware Dies

AGATHA CHRISTIE

Collins Crime Club 1933
artist: **Lambart**

At a supper party, the actress Jane Wilkinson confides in Hercule Poirot that she has 'just got to get rid of' her husband, Lord Edgware. She wants to remarry but her husband refuses to divorce her. The next day Inspector Japp of Scotland Yard arrives to tell Poirot that the wealthy Lord Edgware has been found murdered. For Agatha Christie's *Lord Edgware Dies* Lambart records in blue, black and white the scene as the fourth Baron Edgware lies slumped across his desk in his library. He has been 'stabbed in the back of the neck just at the roots of the hair'. A sombre-looking man, who must surely be Poirot, sits staring at the body.

"Found Drowned"

EDEN PHILLPOTTS

Hutchinson 1931
artist: **unknown**

Eden Phillpotts' *"Found Drowned"* has a particularly colourful wrapper, purple, yellow, red and turquoise. It presents the discovery of a body at the mouth of a cave, with the sea and cliffs of Daleham in the background. 'Where a high tide had deposited the usual fringe of flotsam in a cave, the long-shore man had found a body.' By means of clothing and an unopened letter the remains are identified as those of John Fleming. Drowning is given as the cause of death, but retired surgeon Dr Meredith becomes suspicious and uses his medical knowledge to expose the truth, claiming that 'He was poisoned'. Meredith normally devotes himself to 'reading, contemplation and organic chemistry' – his 'abiding joy' – but also enjoys detection. Eventually, he solves the mystery of the corpse in the cave.

The Marylebone Miser

EDEN PHILLPOTTS

Hutchinson 1926
artist: **C. Morse**

C. Morse has produced an attractive design in red, yellow, green, mauve and brown for *The Marylebone Miser* by Eden Phillpotts. The body of Jarvis Swann, the miser in question, is shown on the floor of his flat, 'a chamber ... more like a steel safe than a dwelling apartment'. Despite being alone in 'an impregnable chamber of steel and stone' with 'no possibility of exit', he has been murdered with 'a heavy knife ... driven through his back, penetrating the heart'. 'Suicide was out of the question and murder certain.' Geraldine and Reginald Swann are shown looking thoughtful in the foreground, after hearing that they are to inherit their uncle's fortune. Retired policeman John Ringrose eventually solves this locked room mystery.

Death in the Quarry

G.D.H. AND M. COLE

Collins Crime Club 1934
artist: **Youngman Carter**

Death in the Quarry is one of the novels in which Superintendent Wilson collaborates with the Hon. Everard Blatchington, who seeks his friend's help when the case demands the professional touch. The explosion so graphically depicted on Youngman Carter's wrapper occurs at the outset of the narrative, while Blatchington and Denis Jordan are walking in the Cotswolds. They are above the quarry of the Attwood Pottery works when James Burdett, the works manager, is blown to bits, murdered obliquely, by remote control: 'There came a rumbling and a roaring almost beneath their feet. The ground shook and quivered; some small pieces of stone seemed to be dancing in the air.'

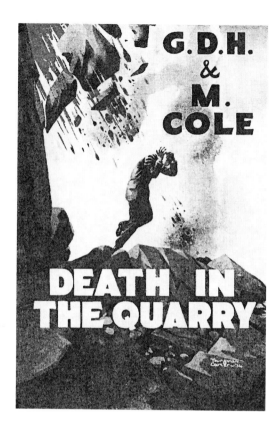

The Man from the River

G.D.H. AND M. COLE

Collins 1928
artist: **J. Morton-Sale**

The Man from the River provides a 'busman's holiday' for Superintendent Henry Wilson, who arrives at Steeple Tollesbury for a restful break, only to run into a murder investigation. His friend, Dr Michael Prendergast, is at hand when the corpse is taken from the River Toll, having 'been in the water for some time'. The victim is William Meston, an unpopular member of a local law firm, with a wife regarded widely as 'the Scarlet Woman' and a partner who has been cooking the books. Since he could 'swim like a duck' and proves to have a broken neck, there is plainly a case to answer. Morton-Sale shows the unfortunate solicitor against a pink sky, before his removal from the water.

The Black Stage
ANTHONY GILBERT

Collins Crime Club 1945
artist: **unknown**

Lewis Bishop is a blackmailer, thief and bigamist and so has wide potential as a perfect murder victim. On a visit to the Vereker family mansion, Four Acres, he suddenly announces that he is going to marry the widow Tessa Goodier and has plans for 'sweeping changes which will affect everyone' in the house. The wrapper for Anthony Gilbert's *The Black Stage* pictures the tense scene in the library after a shot has been heard. In front of the french windows, in a green dress and holding a revolver, is Anne Vereker, 'standing by something dark and dreadful on the carpet', the body of Lewis Bishop. The onlookers are Tessa Goodier and Anne's cousin, Alistair. Anne is arrested and Arthur Crook sets out to prove her innocence.

Relative to Poison
E.C.R. LORAC

Collins Crime Club 1947
artist: **unknown**

In E.C.R. Lorac's *Relative to Poison*, Susan Ferriby and Patricia O'Malley, both recently freed from their wartime jobs, take on the temporary task of looking after the owner of Islip House, the wealthy, arthritic Mrs Roverie. During their second night they are awoken by Mrs Roverie's bell and discover that all the lights have fused and Mrs Roverie is dead. The wrapper has the blonde Patricia and the brunette Susan holding candles and looking down on their dead employer, Patricia in red, Susan in pink. In 'the wonderful curtained bed … the old lady was stretched out stiffly as though every muscle had contracted in a last spasm, her chin jutting up grimly'. Chief-Inspector Macdonald is quickly on the scene and eventually discovers the poisoner.

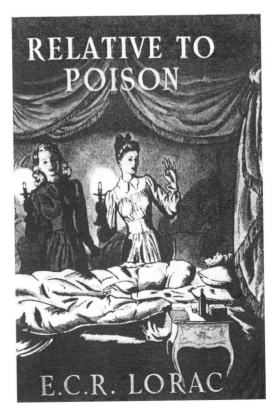

Tour de Force
CHRISTIANNA BRAND

Joseph 1955
artist: **Freda Nichols**

Christianna Brand's thirteen crime novels
include eight classical detective stories,
deservedly famous for their ingenuity and
their last-minute surprises. *Tour de Force*
takes Inspector Cockrill of the Kent County
Police on holiday to a Mediterranean island,
where he becomes involved in the
investigation of the murder of Vanda Lane.
Freda Nichols' effective design exactly
mirrors the description of the dead woman
on the four-poster bed, 'wrapped in a long
white garment like a shroud' and 'laid out
ceremoniously upon a crimson shawl'. 'The
four tall posts, the looped back white
curtains, made of the bed a catafalque.' Her
'dark hair' is 'spread all about her head' and
she has been 'ceremonially laid out, pale
face composed, pale feet placed neatly
together, pale hands loosely clasped' around
'the dagger handle'.

Polly Put the Kettle On
JOAN FLEMING

Hutchinson 1952
artist: **Shirley Hughes**

Joan Fleming's 33 books have great variety
of style and embrace both the traditional
detective story and the modern
psychological crime novel. In *Polly Put the
Kettle On*, George Sudley seeks to start a
new life in the village of Lambing in
Bedfordshire. A victim of love at first
sight, he falls for Polly Edge, who lives at
Hill Farm with her mean husband, Eli,
subsequently found dead in his living
room. Shirley Hughes faithfully records
the scene, in black and white with touches
of grey and red: 'Eli was lying on the
mud-coloured sofa ... His eyes were shut
and one arm was hanging over the side of
the sofa ... There were two cats lying
beside him.' He is thought to have died
from gas poisoning.

The Murder of My Aunt
RICHARD HULL

Faber 1934
artist: **Hookway Cowles**

The Murder of My Aunt is Richard Hull's
first book and it remains a classic example
of the inverted crime novel. The effeminate
and disagreeable Edward Powell decides to
kill his 'spiteful … autocratic and
domineering aunt Mildred', who 'holds the
purse-strings'. To this end he severs eight of
the ten strands of cable which operate the
brakes of her 'antediluvian' Morris.
Hookway Cowles gives us an attractive and
brightly coloured view of the Welsh
countryside, with Mildred Powell in her
car, 'plunging off the road' and
'disappearing over the edge of the bank' to
the dingle below. She has been trying to
avoid hitting Edward's pekingese dog, So-
so, trained by his master to run across the
road at the right moment.
Unfortunately for Edward, his aunt
survives the crash.

Murder isn't Easy
RICHARD HULL

Faber 1936
artist: **Victor Reinganum**

'Richard Hull' is the pseudonym of
Richard Henry Sampson, who specialized
in the inverted novel, where the story is
often told from the murderer's point of
view. *Murder Isn't Easy* is a cautionary tale
for amateur murderers. Three partners run
the advertising agency NeO-aD. The
firm's designer, Nicholas Latimer, decides
to poison its salesman, Paul Spencer,
whose tactlessness is ruining the business:
'Sooner or later he always goes and
quarrels with' the clients. The scene on
Reinganum's brown, blue and white
wrapper shows the dead Paul Spencer,
who has 'fallen forward in his chair,
upsetting the teacup as he did so … since
it lay on the floor'. Nicholas Latimer is
found poisoned in his office at the same
time.

Short List

R. PHILMORE

Collins Crime Club 1938
artist: **unknown**

Short List is set at Radwinter School, where the headmaster is due to retire and the five contenders for his position are assembled. The successful candidate, Rodney Halliday, is prevented by his sudden death from taking up the post, having fallen from 'the balcony over the main door ... that pompous Elizabethan affair, like a Renaissance cardinal's dream', offering a 'wonderful' nocturnal view, with 'the lights and the mines over the valley'. The wrapper depicts Halliday in the course of his descent to 'the asphalt path' below. The detective is C.J. Swan, based by Philmore on C.P. Snow, whom he had taught at Leicester.

Hag's Nook

JOHN DICKSON CARR

Harper 1933
artist: **Frank Dobias**

John Dickson Carr's *Hag's Nook* is the first case for Dr Gideon Fell. The Lincolnshire prison, Starberth, abandoned in 1837, is built around the site of the Hag's Nook gallows. Two generations of the Starberth family have been governors of the prison. Now, the heir to the Starberth estate, Martin, has to spend a night alone in the former Governor's room in order to secure his inheritance. Frank Dobias depicts in orange, blue and white the body of young Martin Starberth falling from the balcony outside the Governor's room in the disused prison. He is discovered 50 feet below with his neck broken. The cunning murder plot is eventually solved by Dr Fell, who observes that 'It's traditional that the Starberths die of broken necks'.

Murder of the Ninth Baronet

J.S. FLETCHER

Harrap 1932
artist: **K.P.**

K.P.'s wrapper for *Murder of the Ninth Baronet*, the fourth of J.S. Fletcher's Ronald Camberwell novels, shows the fall of Sir Stephen Maxtondale from Lady Sybil's Bridge at Heronswood Park, 'a drop of sixty feet'. It seems that 'the bridge had been interfered with' and that 'Nothing could be more certain than that a sudden and fearful death awaited the man who leaned on' a particular rail. Sir Stephen, a man of 'fixed habits', could be relied on to cross the bridge 'every morning', 'regular as clockwork'. He is also found to have died without making a will. Three further murders occur, including the shooting of the Ninth Baronet's brother. Camberwell and Chaney, his partner in detection, get to work on the case.

Dead Men at the Folly

JOHN RHODE

Collins Crime Club 1932
artist: **Ian Hassall**

Dead Men at the Folly is one of the many cases brought by Superintendent Hanslet of Scotland Yard to Dr Priestley in Westbourne Terrace. It involves the deaths of two men, both found dead at the foot of the 'column known as Tilling's Folly', 'on the highest point of Breen Ridge'. The first victim is the 'regular toff' known to the railway staff as 'Gilbert the filbert' and later identified as Captain Godfrey Chaplin. The second is Joe Almond, the 'good-for-nothing brother of the fellow who keeps the Mitre' at Charlton Montague. Ian Hassall offers a grotesque view of one or the other in the course of his fall: probably Almond in his 'breeches and gaiters'.

Wax

ETHEL LINA WHITE

Collins 1935
artist: **Eugene Hastain**

Wax is a characteristic work by Ethel Lina White, an expert in the edgy, neurotic novel designed pleasurably to unsettle its readers. It is set in and around the Riverpool waxworks gallery, a source of obsessive fascination for Sonia Thompson, a young reporter new to the town. In true Gothic fashion, she puts herself at risk, spending a night in the gallery to test the claim that anyone doing so will be found dead the next morning. Hastain's wrapper admirably combines the other-worldly eeriness of the waxworks with the grim, fleshly fact of Alderman Cuttle's corpse, 'lying upon the floor', with 'staring eyes and rigid jaw', in 'a familiar suit of Harris tweed'.

Death in the Diving Pool

CAROL CARNAC

Peter Davies 1940
artist: **J.E.V.**

For Carol Carnac's *Death in the Diving Pool*, J.E.V.'s design in green, black and white is of a hapless hand protruding from the pool beneath the diving board. The scene is partly framed by ivy and running water. Clerewater House is a hotel run by Walter Landon and Anthony Baird. Guests are discussing the disappearance of the jewels of the Rajah of Saripur when Landon comments that he has 'a little notion' of his own. Shortly afterwards he is observed from a distance diving into the hotel pool, but he is not seen to surface. His body forms 'a long dark shadow on the green tiles'. Another body is discovered in the diving pool before Inspector Ryvet of Scotland Yard is called in.

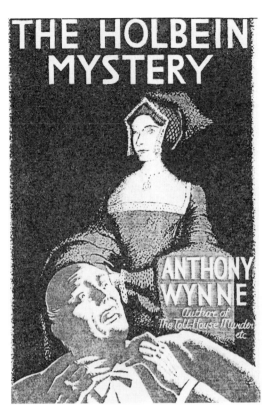

The Holbein Mystery

ANTHONY WYNNE

Hutchinson 1935
artist: **Roberts Johnson**

Anthony Wynne is the author of 27 crime novels, over half of which are impossible crime or locked room mysteries. Roberts Johnson's wrapper for *The Holbein Mystery* portrays Sir Mark Fleet, a Member of Parliament, who is addressing a committee of 30 people when he collapses and dies. Standing alone in front of Holbein's famous picture 'The Red Lady', he suddenly stumbles: 'He clutched at his throat and then threw out his arms … He fell across the table in front of him.' Although there is only 'The Red Lady' behind him, the silver handle of a knife is sticking out of his back. By the time Dr Eustace Hailey starts his investigation, the picture has been stolen: 'The Red Lady' is 'cut out of her frame!'

The Double-Thirteen Mystery

ANTHONY WYNNE

Hutchinson n.d. (1925)
artist: **M.S.E.**

The Double-Thirteen Mystery is the second of Anthony Wynne's novels, all of which have Dr Eustace Hailey, 'the Harley Street Giant', as detective. It is a hectic thriller in his earlier manner, before he came to specialize in impossible crimes. The action involves Russians in exile and the search for the cipher that gives the novel its title. The wrapper features four of the protagonists: the elusive Dr Tsarov of the 'peculiar, glaring eyes'; Olva Vorloff, the femme fatale, whose disappearance brings Dr Hailey into the case; the mysterious 'Mr. Browning' in his 'heavy overcoat with a high collar', with 'a big slouch hat over his eyes'; and the murdered Danatoff, 'struck through the heart' by 'a long knife-blade of the rounded stiletto type'.

By the Author of "THE MYSTERY OF THE EVIL EYE."

The Case of the Constant God

RUFUS KING

Methuen 1938
artist: **unknown**

The Case of the Constant God is a late case for Lieutenant Valcour, a powerful story of revenge, murder and conspiracy to deceive. By so hounding Jenny Alden that she kills herself, Sigurd Repellen becomes the natural enemy of her family, who regard his death at the hands of Jonathan Alden as 'an execution' rather than a murder. The wrapper shows Jenny looking distressed and the packet of letters used to blackmail her. Between them is the fatal encounter described so vividly in the text, when 'Jonathan lifted Repellen by his neck right up into the air and shook him, choking back the inhuman, agonised squeals', 'like the plaints of a terrified rat'.

The Eleven of Diamonds

BAYNARD KENDRICK

Methuen 1937
artist: **Job**

The Eleven of Diamonds is one of three novels featuring Miles Standish Rice, a Deputy Sheriff in Florida, 'long and slender and ... so sunburned' as to appear 'varnished'. Job's eloquent wrapper shows the victim, Edward Fowler, an inveterate gambler, seated in the poker room of the Sunset Bridge Club in Miami, with 'a knife in his heart from the back'. The knife 'looks like it came out of a three-ring circus' and is shaped 'like an anlace' but with a 'heavy hilt'. The eleven of diamonds is heralded by an ominous verse in German, despatched from Amsterdam, and makes its appearance when Fowler is killed, with an unopened pack of cards.

Crime at Christmas

C.H.B. KITCHIN

Hogarth Press 1934
artist: **unknown**

C.H.B. Kitchin wrote only four detective
novels, *Crime at Christmas* being the
second. Malcolm Warren, a young
stockbroker, is the detective in all four
books. Here he is spending Christmas at
Beresford Lodge as a guest of the
Quisberys. A Mrs Harley, the mother of
Quisbery's secretary, is also a guest. At
dinner on Christmas Eve, Warren learns
that she 'suffers terribly from nerves' and
on Christmas morning he finds her dead
on his balcony. She has fallen from the
room above his but her neck has been
broken before her fall. The red wrapper
has a black and white drawing of the
unfortunate woman being strangled.

Middle Class Murder

BRUCE HAMILTON

Methuen 1936
artist: **Job**

Esther Ashwell is married to dentist Tim
Kennedy and their home, The Wilderness,
is on the outskirts of a West Sussex town.
She is 'always very merry in her dark-
haired petite way' but is unfortunately hit
by a lorry, receiving serious injuries which
leave her permanently disfigured. Kennedy
falls in love with an attractive divorcee and
decides that 'Before the summer was out
Esther must die'. Job's design for Bruce
Hamilton's *Middle Class Murder* is blue,
black and white and shows Kennedy
carrying his sleeping wife towards the
open bedroom window on the second
floor of their home, prior to dropping her
45 feet onto a concrete courtyard and so
killing her.

The Man Who Was London

J. KILMENY KEITH

Collins 1925
artist: **Ellen Edwards**

The Man Who Was London is the first detective story written by Lucy Beatrice Malleson and was published under her early pseudonym, 'J. Kilmeny Keith'. She is, of course, most famous for her later books written as 'Anthony Gilbert'. Sir John Ryman is found dead in his library at Streathfield Manor, slumped in a red easy chair, 'with one of the African sacrificial knives buried to the hilt in his heart'. An important document relating to a multi-million pound business deal is missing and a card bearing the inscription 'Nemesis-London' is found in its place. Ellen Edwards' design features Sir John's body and a clock showing two o'clock, the time of his death. The faces of his ward, Eve Chauncey, and her cousin appear on the clock face.

THE MAN WHO WAS LONDON

J. KILMENY KEITH

A fine murder mystery by a new writer.

FREEMAN WILLS CROFTS

MYSTERY IN THE CHANNEL

Mystery in the Channel

FREEMAN WILLS CROFTS

Collins Crime Club 1931
artist: **unknown**

A *Mystery in the Channel* is discovered aboard a pleasure yacht, *The Nymph*, when the captain of a cross-Channel steamer observes the body of 'a tall man … dressed … in a dark grey lounge suit' on its deck. 'He was lying hunched up on his face with his right arm underneath him.' Blood spreads out from the head and a trail of blood leads from the body. The man is later identified as Sydney L. Deeping, vice-chairman of Moxon's General Securities. Moxon, the chairman, is also discovered shot, but no weapon is found on board. The wrapper for this Freeman Wills Crofts novel shows the dead Deeping together with the head of a thoughtful-looking Inspector French, who is to solve the mystery.

In at the Death

DAVID FROME

Skeffington n.d. (1929)
artist: **unknown**

In at the Death introduces Major Gregory Lewis, a former MP turned detective to the gentry. He is called in to investigate the death of Nelson Scoville, which, despite the revolver by his side, proves not to be suicide, since he 'has two wounds', either of which 'would have been mortal'. His mistress, Mimi Dean, is the second victim, found dead in her Park Lane flat by Lewis, who kneels beside her on the wrapper. She lies 'on the soft rose and cream tiles of the bathroom floor', her 'honey-coloured head' hanging 'backwards over the sunken bath', her 'lovely face … hideously swollen and distorted', her 'silken-clad body … grotesquely convulsed'.

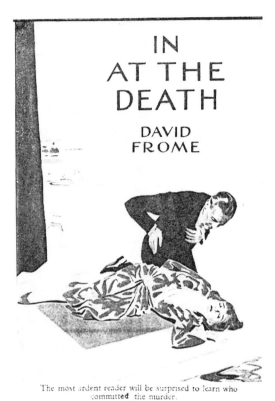

The most ardent reader will be surprised to learn who committed the murder.

A Shilling for Candles

JOSEPHINE TEY

Methuen 1936
artist: **Nick**

Elizabeth Mackintosh used two pseudonyms for her detective novels: 'Gordon Daviot' for her first and 'Josephine Tey' for her other seven. *A Shilling for Candles* is her second, one of six which feature the gentlemanly Inspector Alan Grant of Scotland Yard. Nick paints the scene of William Potticary's discovery: of the body of a woman lying on the beach near Westover. She wears 'a bright green bathing dress' and, on her ankle, a 'chain of platinum links', each 'shaped like a C'. The body is identified as that of the popular film actress, Christine Clay, who bequeathes a shilling for candles to her brother.

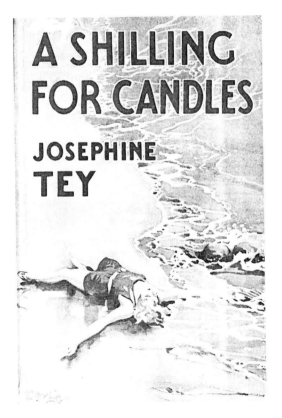

The Bowstring Murders

CARTER DICKSON

Heinemann 1934
artist: **Youngman Carter**

The Bowstring Murders is the first book
written by John Dickson Carr under his
Carter Dickson pseudonym (though it
appeared in America as by 'Carr Dickson').
Henry Steyne is the holder of the Barony
of Rayle, heir to a 15th-century castle,
Bowstring, on the East Anglian coast. He
is a small man who often wears a white-
wool monk's robe and he has the finest
collection of mediaeval arms and armour
in the world. Youngman Carter shows his
murdered body lying in the Armour Hall,
painting the scene in black, white and red.
He lies 'beneath a pedestal-base above
which reared a gigantic armoured dummy
on an armoured wooden horse'. Lord
Rayle has been strangled, yet no one has
entered or left the hall.

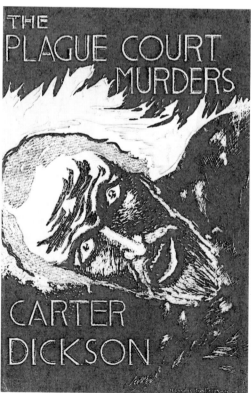

The Plague Court Murders

CARTER DICKSON

Heinemann 1935
artist: **H. Charles Tomlinson**

The Plague Court Murders is the first Sir
Henry Merrivale mystery by Carter
Dickson. A house in Plague Court is
haunted and Roger Darworth, a psychic, is
called in to exorcize the ghost. The
exorcism is performed by Darworth in a
locked stone outhouse, but an alarm bell
summons help and the door is broken
open. Roger Darworth is revealed in the
position shown on Tomlinson's black, red
and white wrapper, lying with his head
almost among the embers of a fire: 'blood
had run down over his face, past the teeth
of the wide-open mouth now wrenched
back in agony'. His body has been 'hacked
like a dummy at bayonet practice', yet
nothing could have entered or left the
room.

The Man in the Brown Suit

AGATHA CHRISTIE

Bodley Head 1924
artist: **unknown**

Anne Beddingfield has walked to the end of the platform at the Hyde Park Corner tube station. She passes a man smelling of mothballs, 'standing close to the edge of the tunnel ... a small, thin man, very brown of face, with light blue eyes'. He turns, looks beyond Anne and his face becomes distorted with fear: 'He took a step backwards as though involuntarily recoiling from some danger'. He falls off the platform onto the live rail, from which officials lift him back onto the platform. Anne watches as a tall man in a brown suit, who claims to be a doctor, suddenly appears, bending over the body to examine it. It is this scene which appears on the wrapper of Agatha Christie's *The Man in the Brown Suit*. [See colour section, page (f).]

Death in the Stocks

GEORGETTE HEYER

Longmans, Green 1935
artist: **Thorpe**

Georgette Heyer's *Death in the Stocks* opens just after midnight on Ashleigh Green, which is surrounded by cottages. The stocks are a feature of the green and are illuminated by moonlight as Police-Constable Dickenson pedals past on his bicycle. He is surprised to see that 'a gentleman in evening dress' is sitting in the stocks, 'apparently asleep, for his body had sagged forward, his head lolling on his chest', as illustrated by Thorpe. On investigating, he discovers the dead body of Arnold Vereker, stabbed in the back. Vereker had lived in London but owned Riverside Cottage, which he had used at weekends. Superintendent Hannasyde from Scotland Yard soon discovers that several people have motives for the murder and no alibis. [See colour section, page (f).]

The Castleford Conundrum

J.J. CONNINGTON

Hodder & Stoughton 1932
artist: **E.P.K.**

The Castleford Conundrum brings Sir Clinton Driffield belatedly into a tense domestic tangle, bristling with envy, malice, resentment and fear. The victim is the wealthy Winifred Castleford, whom he recalls from *Mystery at Lynden Sands*. She dies intestate, having destroyed her existing will and failed to endorse a new one. The handsome wrapper shows her slumped in a 'rustic arm-chair' on the veranda at the Chalet, where she has been painting. Nearby is 'the easel, with its half-finished picture. On the ground beside it lay the wooden sketching-box'. Beyond these is 'the little square cane table which carried the tea-things'. The man disappearing from view has taken fright at the sight of the body. [See colour section, page (f).]

The Case of the Hanging Rope

CHRISTOPHER BUSH

Cassell 1937
artist: **unknown**

The Case of the Hanging Rope is sufficiently complex for a family tree of those involved to be provided as a preliminary. The man on the vibrant wrapper is a victim of the murderer obliquely only, in that he is intended to hang for his wife's murder. Her death on her wedding night is Ludovic Travers' major concern but the bridegroom also poses a problem. He lies in a drugged sleep, 'sprawled diagonally', his 'cheeks a yellowish grey, his eyes bagged, mouth gaping and hairy chest bulging through the wide opening of dressing-gown and pyjama jacket'. Hanging from 'a crossbeam of old oak' is a rope 'the thickness of stout linen-line'. [See colour section, page (f).]

Post after Post Mortem

E.C.R. LORAC

Collins Crime Club 1936
artist: **unknown**

Ruth Surray finds that her work as a writer
renews rather than drains her vitality. None
the less, she is found dead during a visit to
her parents' home, Upwood House.
Professor and Mrs Surray discover their
daughter's dead body in 'the sunny
bedroom where Ruth lay like a child, still
and untroubled, her white face smiling the
strange peaceful smile of death, and a box
of sleeping-draught tablets on the table
beside her'. This scene is clearly illustrated
on the wrapper for E.C.R. Lorac's *Post after
Post Mortem*. Under the red pill box are two
papers, a signed but unwitnessed draft of
her will and what could be a suicide note.
Her brother Richard, a psychologist takes a
letter written by Ruth on the night of her
death to Chief-Inspector Macdonald, who
doubts the inquest verdict of suicide after
reading it. [See colour section, page (g).]

Murder at Wrides Park

J.S. FLETCHER

Harrap 1931
artist: **Nick**

Nick's dramatic nocturnal scene for J.S.
Fletcher's *Murder at Wrides Park* shows the
blackmailer Dengo clutching the air in
agony after being run 'clean through the
heart' in Middle Spinney at Wrides Park,
the estate of Mr Nicholas. A swordstick
belonging to Mr Nicholas is found hidden
at the scene of the crime and dominates
the foreground of the wrapper. It seems a
straightforward case of a blackmail victim's
turning murderer, but Ronald
Camberwell, in his first investigation, finds
that all is not so simple. Camberwell has
recently become Mr Nicholas' companion
and now goes to his defence with the help
of ex-CID officer Chaney. They discover,
among other things, that Dengo is an
anagram of the victim's real name, Ogden.
[See colour section, page (g).]

The Hanging Captain

HENRY WADE

Constable 1932
artist: **M. Crichton**

Gerald Sterron and the butler, Willing,
break open the study door at Ferris Court
to discover the room 'in darkness, save for
a small reading-lamp which cast a dull red
glow upon the writing-table'. Their eyes
are 'fixed in stupefied horror upon a body
which hung against the curtain of the
further window'. The corpse is that of
former Dragoon captain Herbert Sterron,
brother of Gerald and owner of Ferris
Court. The cord from which *The Hanging
Captain* swings hangs from the curtain
pole, 'one end fastened to the man's neck
and the other to a radiator which stood in
the window'. M. Crichton perfectly
captures this scene from Henry Wade's
novel, which goes on to recount the
police investigation of this country house
murder. [See colour section, page (g).]

The Murder of Mrs. Davenport

ANTHONY GILBERT

Collins 1928
artist: **C. Morse**

In Anthony Gilbert's *The Murder of Mrs.
Davenport*, Sir Denis Brinsley is confronted
on the eve of his marriage by the beautiful
Mrs Helen Davenport. Using his indiscreet
letters to her, written 14 years earlier, she
tries to blackmail him. Morse accurately
portrays the later discovery of Mrs
Davenport's body, 'straggled on the sofa',
with 'dreadful protruding eyes, the
swollen, blackened tongue in the open
mouth … the ominous marks on her long
and lovely throat'. She lies 'from the waist
to the feet … on the brown velvet couch,
but her head and one arm dragged almost
to the floor'. The 'method of her death' is
'indisputable'. Morse also shows the
shadow of her murderer. [See colour
section, page (g).]

8
A Variety of Weapons

A Variety of Weapons

RUFUS KING

Doubleday Crime Club 1943
artist: **Leo Manso**

A Variety of Weapons begins with Anne Ledrick's assignment to photograph 'Estelle Marlow's beloved ocelots'. Over the years, someone has used a variety of weapons to murder members and friends of the Marlow family; and Manso shows the gun with which Jerry Abbott 'tripped and blew the top of his head off', 'the jar of foie gras' that poisoned Frank Lawrence and the 'Cellini dagger' with which Alice Marlow was stabbed. Most chilling of all is the photograph of the ocelot, bearing the evidence of Justin Marlow's radium poisoning. He has held the negatives of Anne's photographs and each exposure shows 'the silvery skeleton of the bones of [his] hand'.

The Glass Key

DASHIELL HAMMETT

Cassell 1931
artist: **unknown**

Dashiell Hammett was a trail-blazer of the American detective novel, breaking new ground with his abrasive style and blunt, earthy language. His books are populated with realistic characters and their violence is often spectacular. Underlying all the gunfire and flying fists is an implacable hatred of corruption. *The Glass Key* is a story of political corruption featuring Ned Beaumont, a heavy-drinking gambler, tall, slim, moustached, faithful to his friends and devoted to his boss, the politician, Paul Madvig. The wrapper shows him at a decisive moment in the action, having 'moved his hand sideways until [his] pistol was pointed at [his antagonist's] belly'. He intends to claim having acted in self-defence.

Beginning with a Bash
ALICE TILTON

Collins Crime Club 1937
artist: **unknown**

Beginning with a Bash is the first of the Leonidas Witherall mysteries, written by Phoebe Atwood Taylor under the pseudonym 'Alice Tilton'. Like the Asey Mayo series, they are clever and intricate, remarkable as much for elaborate action as for high spirits. The victim of the hammer blow depicted on the yellow wrapper is Professor John North, 'an eminent anthropologist', felled in Dot Peters' Boston bookstore on a 'below zero' day. The killer has judged the blow exactly, striking 'square on the base of the skull', 'Not too hard to be too messy, not too soft so the fellow'd only be stunned'. The weapon is Jonas Peters' 'rounding hammer', used 'for pounding and rounding the backs of books'.

Murder in the Squire's Pew
J.S. FLETCHER

Harrap 1932
artist: **Nick**

Murder in the Squire's Pew is the third case for J.S. Fletcher's detective Ronald Camberwell. Nick's wrapper shows Linwood church from which priceless antiques have been stolen, with the murder weapon in the foreground. Canon Effingham calls in Camberwell and his partner Chaney to investigate. The case takes on a more serious aspect with the discovery in the Squire's pew at Linwood of the dead body of Dick Skate. Chaney soon discovers the weapon, moving 'quickly forward to pick up from a flower-bed something which had suddenly glittered in a shaft of sunlight': '"A spanner!" he said. "Brand new and stainless … except for these specks … see what it is, Camberwell? Blood!"'

Ground for Suspicion

MILES BURTON

Collins Crime Club 1950
artist: **N. Manwaring**

Ground for Suspicion is set in Shellmouth, a genteel seaside resort, to which Desmond Merrion takes his wife Mavis for an early holiday. This puts him well ahead of the game when Inspector Arnold arrives to investigate the latest in a series of sudden deaths in the town. Colonel Delabole collapses during a public meeting; Mrs Worthing dies in her sleep; and Miss Bircham is strangled. Manwaring's handsome wrapper shows the colonel with the exploding firecracker that causes such confusion at the moment of his death. Also shown is the 'aural aid' which proves to have contained 'apparatus capable of causing the injuries found to have been inflicted on the dead man's brain'.

Murder in the Coal Hole

MILES BURTON

Collins Crime Club 1940
artist: **James E. McConnell**

McConnell's tan, olive green and black composition for Miles Burton's *Murder in the Coal Hole* shows Polesworth, the unpopular manager of Middleden Elementary School, about to meet his fate in the coal cellar. He is later found by Mrs Day, the cleaner, 'Sitting on the floor with his legs outspread and his back reclining gracefully against the heap of coals'. By this time he is dead, killed by carbon monoxide poisoning from a gas bracket that is turned full on. Inspector Arnold of Scotland Yard and his friend Desmond Merrion carry out a complex investigation during which the murderer makes 'as many false trails as he could think of'. Eventually they discover who has knocked Polesworth unconscious and left him to die.

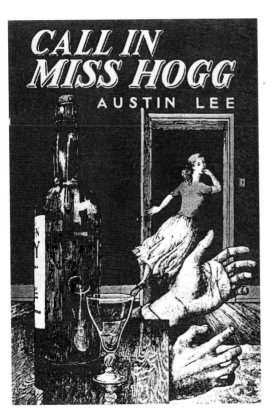

Call in Miss Hogg

AUSTIN LEE

Cape 1956
artist: **William McLaren**

Call in Miss Hogg is the second of the nine
cases of Flora Hogg, the former
schoolmistress turned private detective.
She and Milly Brown are present at a party
when a young man is poisoned in a
neighbouring apartment. McLaren's
meticulous blue and orange wrapper shows
Mervyn Lloyd's hands as he writhes on the
floor, after drinking sherry containing an
'irritant poison'. At the door, Hazel
Wright, a fledgling actress, rushes for help.
On the table are 'a bottle of sherry ...
rather less than half full and a single glass,
which had a few dregs at the bottom'.

Not to Be Taken

ANTHONY BERKELEY

Hodder & Stoughton 1938
artist: **unknown**

Anthony Berkeley's *Not to Be Taken* deals
with the murder of John Waterhouse in
the Dorset village of Anneypenney, to
which he had retired from a career which
had taken him around the world. Despite
an absence of apparent enemies, arsenic has
somehow found its way into his system.
The blue and cream wrapper has 28 dark
blue bottles of poison neatly arranged on
four shelves, against a pale blue
background. Each bottle bears an identical
cream and red poison label. 'Only the
habit-forming drugs like cocaine and
morphia' are required 'to be entered in a
doctor's poison-book'. Arsenic, like
strychnine and cyanide and 'the other Part
I, Schedule I poisons', does not.

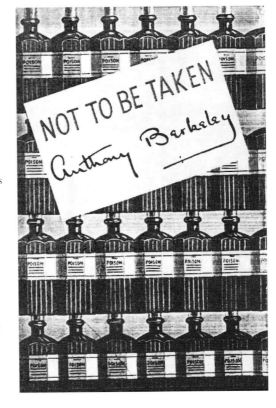

A Taste for Honey
GERALD HEARD

Cassell 1942
artist: **unknown**

A Taste for Honey is the first of three
eccentric novels in which Gerald Heard
revives the elderly Sherlock Holmes,
renaming him 'Mr Bowcross' in Britain,
'Mr Mycroft' in America. The narrator is
Sydney Silchester, a natural recluse who
regards his fellow men as 'rather a
nuisance'. His taste for honey induces him
to break his rule of solitude and call on his
beekeeping neighbours, including Mr
Bowcross, to whom he eventually owes
his life. The wrapper shows one of Mr
Heregrove's 'miniature monsters', each
with its 'super-sting', curving round 'until
it seemed it would pierce through the
chitin mail of the … insect's own thorax'.
The green skull prepares us for the power
they wield.

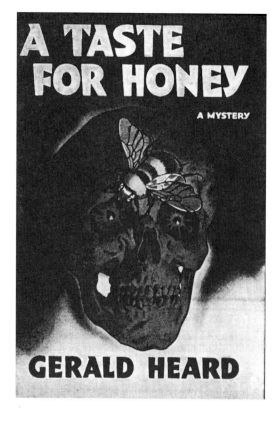

Sparkling Cyanide
AGATHA CHRISTIE

Collins Crime Club 1945
artist: **Leslie Stead**

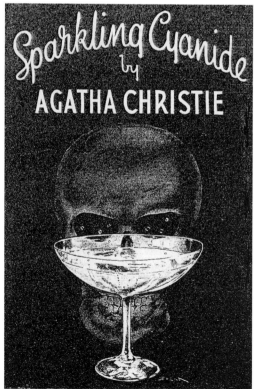

Rosemary Barton is thought to have
committed suicide by cyanide poisoning
during an evening party at a London
restaurant, a year before the opening of
Agatha Christie's *Sparkling Cyanide*. One
year later, a second party takes place, with
the same six people who had sat there on
the earlier occasion, again ranged round a
table. The name 'Rosemary' means
'remembrance' and, inevitably, it is of
Rosemary that they are thinking. They are
all on edge, waiting for something to
happen. After drinking champagne George
Barton slumps 'down in his chair … his
face turning purple as he fought for
breath'. 'It took him a minute and a half to
die.' Stead's design features a ghastly green
skull grinning behind a glass of sparkling
champagne, laced with cyanide.

Damsels in Distress

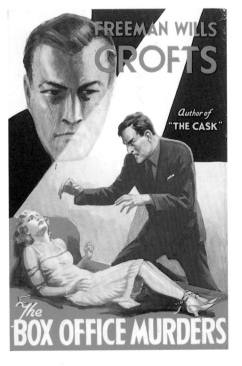

Distraught Men

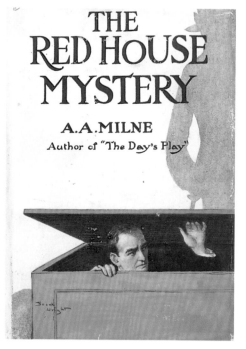

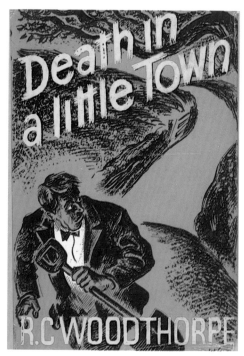

Scene of the Crime

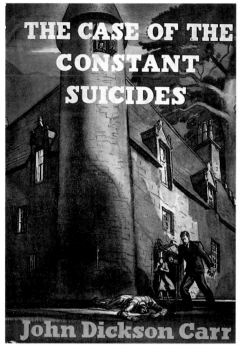

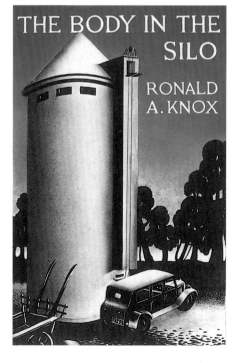

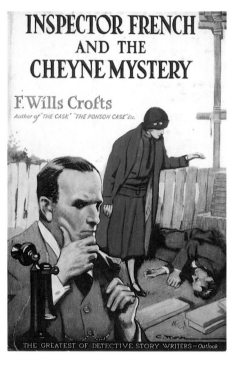

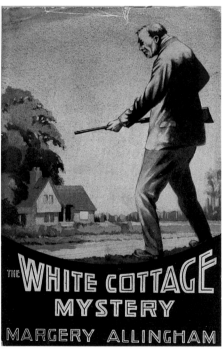

The Watchers

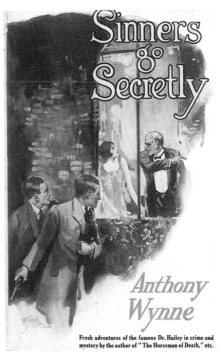

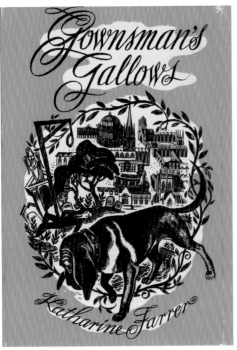

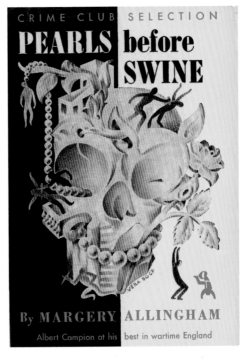

Creatures in Crime

The Victims

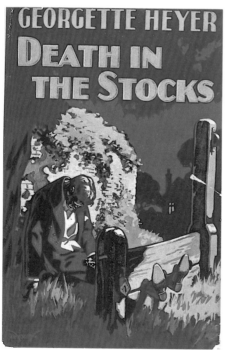

The Victims

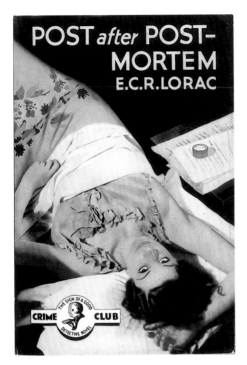

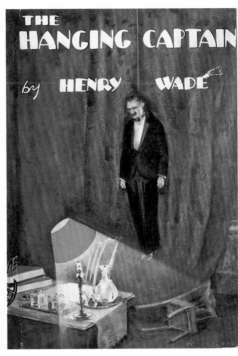

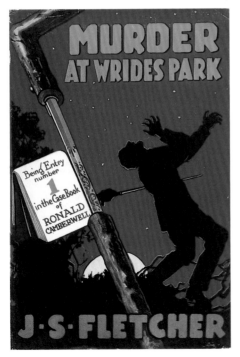

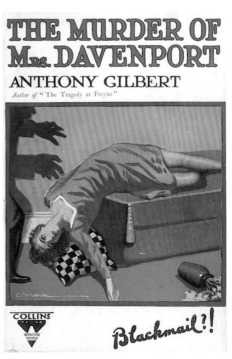

Arm of the Law

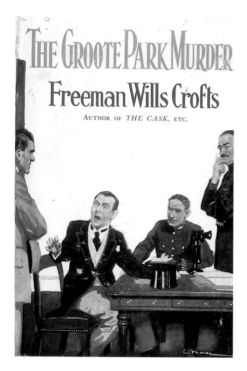

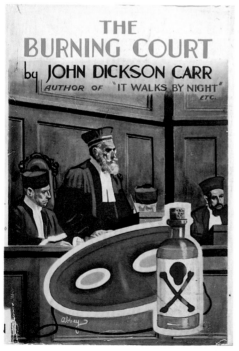

The Detectives

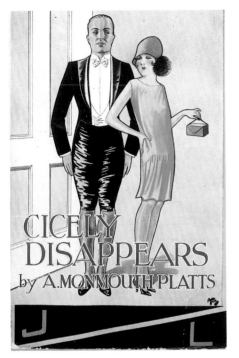

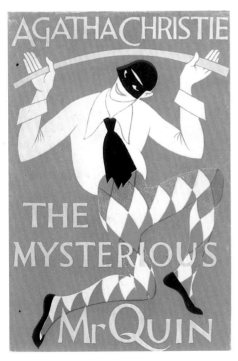

The Clues

Murder on the Move

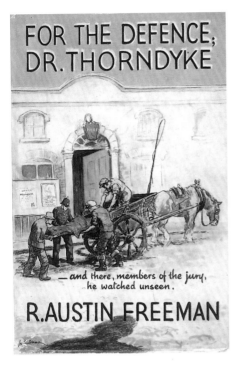

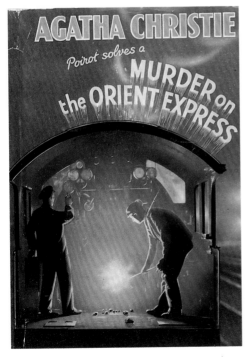

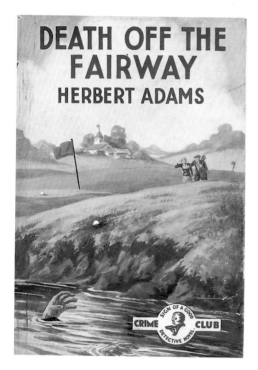

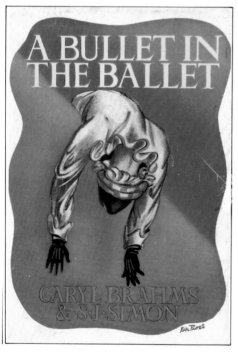

Three at Wolfe's Door
REX STOUT

Collins Crime Club 1961
artist: **William Randell**

Three at Wolfe's Door contains three Nero Wolfe novellas, each with its individual method of murder. In 'Poison a la Carte', Wolfe's own chef, Fritz Brenner, cooks a gourmet dinner at which Vincent Pyle dies from arsenic on the blinis. In 'Method Three for Murder', Phoebe Arden is found dead in a New York taxi with a 'knife whose handle was perpendicular to her ribs' stuck 'all the way in'. It is 'an ordinary kitchen knife with a five-inch blade and a plastic handle'. In 'The Rodeo Murder', Wade Eisler dies during the World Series Rodeo, of which he is 'chief backer'. Cal Barrow's rope is 'wound around his throat so many times … that his chin was pushed up'.

Legacy of Death
MILES BURTON

Collins Crime Club 1960
artist: **William Randell**

Legacy of Death is a very late case for Inspector Arnold and Desmond Merrion, who have nearly 30 years of shared criminal investigation behind them at this stage of their careers. The scene is Forest House, a residential home for elderly people, two of whom are murdered for the same substantial fortune. A nurse at the home is also killed, by an amazingly reckless and elaborate trick. Randell's wrapper shows the murderer in the act of doctoring Henry Corfe's nightcap by adding 'Smith's Aphicide … in liquid form … to the whisky which was left in the bottle'. Merrion reconstructs the scene, explaining, as so often, to the less perceptive and imaginative Arnold.

Cop Hater

ED MCBAIN

Boardman 1958
artist: **Denis McLoughlin**

Cop Hater is the first of over 40 books by
Evan Hunter, writing as Ed McBain,
featuring officers of the 87th Precinct in an
imaginary city, similar to New York. Two
policemen have been shot dead and
Detective Steve Carella is looking for a
man with a grudge against the police and a
.45 automatic. Denis McLoughlin shows
the murder of Detective Hank Bush by
the 'man with the .45' waiting 'in the
shadows', his black clothes blending him
'with the void of the alley mouth': 'His
hand tightened … a .45 automatic spat
orange flame into the night, once, twice,
again, again … he saw the cop clutch at
his chest and fall for the pavement'.

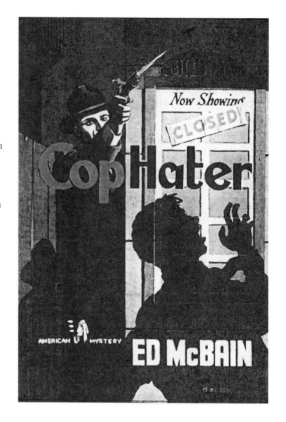

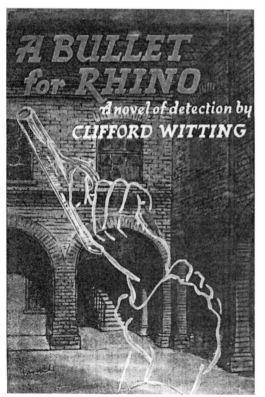

A Bullet for Rhino

CLIFFORD WITTING

Hodder & Stoughton 1950
artist: **Wardill**

Clifford Witting published 16 well-made,
old-fashioned English detective novels. *A
Bullet for Rhino* is the ninth case for
Inspector Harry Charlton. He is present
when the Old Boys' Cricket Match at
Mereworth School is marred by the
murder of war hero Colonel Rhino
Garstang, shot that evening. Wardill's
design shows the cloisters at Mereworth,
with the stone steps leading up to 'D'
dormitory, where Garstang was
accommodated. In the foreground, two
hands struggle for possession of a gun.
After the colonel's antagonist has 'jumped
at him, clutched desperately at his wrist
and twisted it with all his strength', there is
'an explosion' and the colonel, 'shot
through the brain', falls dead. On the
ground, 'close to his right knee' is 'his
Browning self-loader'.

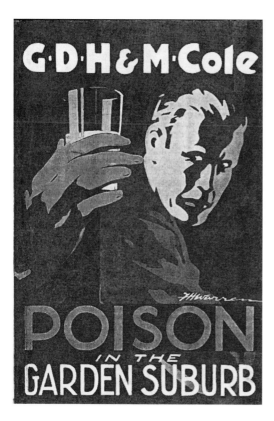

Poison in the Garden Suburb

G.D.H AND M. COLE

Collins 1929
artist: **F.H. Warren**

Poison in the Garden Suburb is an early case for Henry Wilson, during his time as a private investigator. It opens at a meeting of the Medstead Literary Institute, in the course of which Harold Cayley collapses while addressing the assembled company. He utters 'a horrible, choking cry' and crashes to the floor 'in the grip of some appalling spasm'. No one is allowed to leave the hall, since 'there is no doubt that he has been poisoned, and within the last hour or so'. F.H. Warren's wrapper shows the glass of lemonade in which 15 grains of strychnine were administered. The anxious-looking man is perhaps the victim, but there are other possibilities.

And Where's Mr. Bellamy?

STUART MARY WICK

Hutchinson n.d. (1948)
artist: **Tansley**

And Where's Mr. Bellamy? opens in the 1940s but largely harks back to the late-Victorian era, when Teddy Branksome was a small boy. Despite the pseudonym 'Stuart Mary Wick', the author is Kathleen Freeman, already well established as 'Mary Fitt' when this book was published. It is a powerful story of murder and revenge, with Mr Bellamy as the cat among the pigeons. The victim dies a 'slow death', brought about 'by dose after calculated dose of one of the cruellest of poisons', administered 'in a form disguised as loving attention to her wishes'. Tansley's wrapper shows the plate of maids-of-honour onto which the arsenic is poured.

Knife in the Dark

G.D.H. AND M. COLE

Collins Crime Club 1941
artist: **Leslie Stead**

Knife in the Dark is the only full-length
case of Mrs Elizabeth Warrender, who
otherwise figures exclusively in stories. She
is visiting the university town of Stamford
with her detective son James when her
hostess, Kitty Lake, is murdered at the
undergraduate dance she has organized.
The killer has stabbed 'in the left centre of
her naked back' with 'an odd sort of knife,
antique or curio of some kind – pretty
heavily carved', its handle of a 'rough-
carved metal that won't take any prints'.
Stead's misty blue wrapper has a
background of university towers with, to
the left, the bloodstained knife, forming
the upright of the 'K' in the title.

Death of a Queen

C. ST JOHN SPRIGG

Nelson 1935
artist: **C. Walter Hodges**

Death of a Queen is an unusual case for
Charles Venables, the upper-crust
journalist who figures in three of C. St
John Sprigg's novels. He is persuaded to
visit Iconia, a small Balkan border country
'trapped between the Danube and the
Transylvanian Alps', where the royal
family, under threat, has need of his
detective skills. C. Walter Hodges'
dramatic red wrapper shows Queen Hanna
the morning after her all-night vigil for
'the Feast of St Buron', 'lying athwart the
prie-dieu in her huge bedroom …
strangled by the same silken cord which …
had first stained the Herzegovin blood
with a fratricidal crime'. Framing the scene
is the cause of her death, the self-same
cord 'with which Augustus the Clerk and
his five children were throttled'.

Constable Guard Thyself!

HENRY WADE

Constable 1934
artist: **Youngman Carter**

Henry Wade wrote 20 quintessentially English crime novels. In *Constable Guard Thyself!*, Captain Scole, Chief Constable of Brodshire, is found in his office, mysteriously shot. Scotland Yard's Inspector John Poole is called in to unravel the mystery. Youngman Carter's carefully detailed wrapper shows various documents: Albert Hinde's letter to the Chief Constable, in 'shaky and sprawling' handwriting; an anonymous letter 'in connection with contracts for police uniforms'; a telegram sent to Scotland Yard; and a note with a pin through it, 'in Captain Scole's hand'. An automatic pistol and two bullets with their brass cartridge cases rest on the documents. The pistol is of the type that ejects its cartridge cases 'to the right'.

The Gun in Daniel Webster's Bust

MARGARET SCHERF

Doubleday Crime Club 1949
artist: **Vera Bock**

The Gun in Daniel Webster's Bust is the first of Margaret Scherf's series about Henry Bryce and Emily Murdock, later his wife. Emily owns the Lentement Decorating Company in New York and Henry is her assistant. When Cleo Delaphine is 'shot from a revolver at close range', the weapon is not 'found on the scene'. Instead, with 'a rattle and a metallic thump', it falls from the bust of Daniel Webster that has 'rested for the last three years on the shelf of a Queen Anne bookcase' in Emily's studio. Vera Bock's exuberant wrapper shows the gun poised over the one-eared bust, which is draped with a 'fur scarf' (deputizing, with acknowledged 'artistic licence', for the mink cape of the narrative).

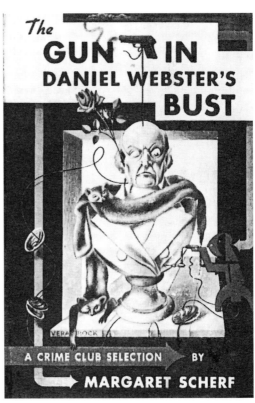

The Shudders

ANTHONY ABBOT

Farrar & Rinehart 1943
artist: **Robert Graves**

The Shudders, despite its publication date, deals with a fantastic sequence of events occurring in 1936, before Thatcher Colt's marriage to Florence Dunbar. He locks horns with the most dangerous of modern criminals, the sinister Dr Baldwin, who has found a new way to kill people without leaving any trace. Robert Graves' grim blue wrapper shows the 'picture of Dr Baldwin' drawn by Colt during an interview with him, described by Tony Abbott as 'a surrealist's sketch of Baldwin's soul … uncanny … malevolent … and yet … cowering, frightened and obscurely pitiful'. The hypodermic is not used to administer the means of death but, with bizarre and terrible consequences, for quite another purpose.

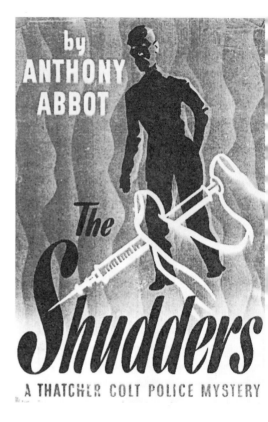

The Judas Window

CARTER DICKSON

Heinemann 1938
artist: **Youngman Carter**

As 'Carter Dickson', John Dickson Carr produced a classic locked room problem in *The Judas Window.* James Answell awakes from a drugged sleep to find himself locked in Avory Hume's study with the dead body of his host. Youngman Carter's design is dark pink and black on white and shows Hume's corpse lying on its back near the window. 'At the end of the arrow, which had been driven eight inches into Hume's heart, were attached three bedraggled and dusty feathers.' Sir Henry Merrivale, Answell's Defence Counsel, maintains that the fatal injury could only have been inflicted if the arrow 'had been put into the groove of a crossbow and fired'. The crossbow brought by H.M. to court appears in dark pink on the wrapper.

9
An Inquiry

The Bedford Row Mystery

J.S. FLETCHER

Hodder & Stoughton 1925
artist: **unknown**

'Bedford Row, on the western edge of Gray's Inn, is well known to all Londoners as being chiefly the business abode of limbs of the law'. So begins J.S. Fletcher's *The Bedford Row Mystery*. Solicitor Henry Marchmont, who has lived above his office for many years, is discovered on his staircase, shot through the heart. Detective-Sergeant Liversedge of Scotland Yard leads an inquiry to discover whose arm aimed the revolver seen pointed at Marchmont from a ground-floor room by Miss Sanderthwaite, a crazy old spinster. During the investigation, suspicion falls on several people, all depicted on the wrapper: the wealthy John Lonsdale and his daughter Angelita; the Chancery Lane lawyers Crench and Garner; and the managing clerk Hemingway Simpson.

Oddways

HERBERT ADAMS

Methuen 1930
artist: **Frank Marston**

In Herbert Adams' *Oddways*, two brothers, Sidney and Frederick Ankaret, are murdered on the same night, at the same hour, but 40 miles apart. Frank Marston's wrapper design is composed of a white question mark made up of suspects, witnesses, gallows and victim, all black against a blue background. Nan Lockwood stands 'beside the dead body of Sidney Ankaret, holding in her hand one of her own knives'. Jean Auriol, Frederick's chauffeur, hurries to a motor-cycle on which he rides 'back to Henley' and fires 'two shots, either of which would have been fatal'. The postman, 'just due for the last delivery of letters', is shot at by Auriol, who misses him: he recovers and goes on 'to the next house, Oddways'.

Police at the Funeral

MARGERY ALLINGHAM

Heinemann 1931
artist: **Youngman Carter**

The setting for Margery Allingham's *Police at the Funeral* is an old house, Socrates Close, at Cambridge. Here reside an elderly widow, Mrs Caroline Faraday, and her three middle-aged children. Three members of Mrs Faraday's family die by violence: her nephew, Andrew Seeley, is found 'bound hand and foot with cord and with a bullet wound in his head' in the River Granta; her daughter Julia and another nephew, George Faraday, are found dead from poison. Youngman Carter designed most of the wrappers for his wife's books. Here he makes a fanciful question mark from the coffins of the three victims, borne in funeral procession and accompanied by the police. Inspector Stanislaus Oates and Albert Campion make the necessary inquiries.

Death in Five Boxes

CARTER DICKSON

Heinemann 1938
artist: **Youngman Carter**

Carter Dickson's *Death in Five Boxes* is another mystifying problem for Sir Henry Merrivale, beginning with the discovery of four guests in various stages of atropine poisoning, with their host, Felix Haye, stabbed through the back with a sword stick. As if anticipating his death, Haye has deposited with a firm of London lawyers five small parcels containing 'evidence about certain persons who wished him dead'. Youngman Carter's stylish design – in brown, black and white – depicts the five packages, each 'a cardboard box about six inches long by four inches broad', 'wrapped in heavy brown paper, tied with strong string, and sealed in two places with red wax'.

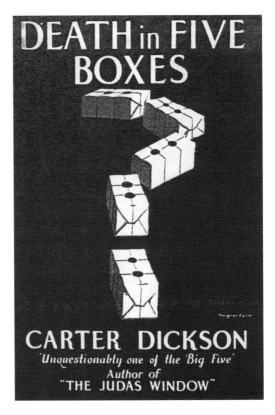

10
Arm of the Law

The Lucky Policeman
RUPERT PENNY

Collins Crime Club 1938
artist: **unknown**

The Lucky Policeman is Chief-Inspector
Edward Bede, who has 'a touching faith in
human behaviour'. Rupert Penny's eight
'Policeman' novels were published over a
period of six years and all feature C.I.
Bede. The bold wrapper for *The Lucky
Policeman* has a copper-coloured old penny,
embossed with the head of a policeman
and set against a blue background. Bede
has here to deal with a rapid succession of
murders in the New Forest, including that
of Prudence Hill, who is dealt 'a heavy
blow on the back of her head' before her
face is pressed 'down into the soft earth'.
In each case the victim's left shoe is
missing.

The Cat Jumps
MILES BURTON

Collins Crime Club 1946
artist: **S. Herbert**

The Cat Jumps is vintage middle-period
Burton, clever, composed and absorbing. It
begins with the wounding of a horse,
sufficient in itself to put the expression of
'utter bewilderment' onto the face of
Sergeant Neatshead, whose imposing
portrait by S. Herbert occupies the
wrapper. The windows are those of Mrs
Cottington's dining-room and the knife is
either that which murdered her or that
which stabbed the horse: they are 'exactly
similar ... in every detail'. Sadly, the cat
Belisarius does not appear.

Man Dead

SELWYN JEPSON

Collins Crime Club 1951
artist: **unknown**

Man Dead is a concentrated, hectic thriller that might have found its ideal incarnation as a glossy film melodrama. By organizing the removal of her murdered lover from her home, Sarah Gray puts herself outside the law and becomes vulnerable to blackmail. The wrapper portrait of her dead father, Lord Justice Gray, effectively oversees the action, soothing Sarah with its 'gentle, wise melancholy' and reducing a blackmailer 'from self-assurance to near terror'. Though 'he administered the Law', he was 'the most human of human beings' and would have felt that his daughter had 'done wrong in breaking laws but right in trying to serve the spirit and purpose of them'.

The Second Man

EDWARD GRIERSON

Chatto & Windus 1956
artist: **Stratton**

Edward Grierson was a barrister who wrote four authoritative crime novels, the second of which is *The Second Man*. Marion Kerrison is beginning to make a name for herself at the Bar when she is given the defence brief in a murder case, Regina v. Maudsley. The defendant, John Maudsley, is accused of murdering his aunt, but Marion is convinced of his innocence, despite his unhelpful behaviour. Stratton's red wrapper shows Mr Justice Lorne intently watching Marion, who 'always appeared her best in a wig and gown, with her hair hidden and the Gothic set of her face against the white curls'. She also has 'beautiful hands', which 'showed up well with the black of the gown'.

Each Man's Destiny

MAURICE PROCTER

Longmans, Green 1947
artist: **unknown**

Each Man's Destiny is the second of Maurice Procter's 26 crime novels. In it he describes the careers of several young constables in a Lancashire industrial town. The wrapper is blue, pink and black on white and features three policemen, standing under a street lamp in Broomhill, 'a hard town to police'. Constable Mansel stands 'with his thumbs hooked in his night-duty belt', while Sergeant Earle Coffin 'reflected sourly: Trust a police constable not to be late at the last point before home'. Procter shows how the constables react differently to the exacting demands of their profession, the stern discipline, the heavy impositions on private life. Most adapt very well, some become disillusioned and some meet disaster.

No Proud Chivalry

MAURICE PROCTER

Longmans, Green 1947
artist: **unknown**

A line of caped policemen marches smartly out of Otterburn's red brick police station on the red, white and blue wrapper for *No Proud Chivalry*. 'The night inspector came and surveyed them with a professional frown, then they marched out of the building in the old Metropolitan style'. Maurice Procter, himself a former policeman, provides a realistic treatment of police work in this, his first novel. The book traces the progress of Pierce Rogan from the day he joins the Otterburn Borough Police. He soon realizes that the service makes demands on its men that extend even to their private lives. Normal scruples often have to be abandoned in the struggle for promotion.

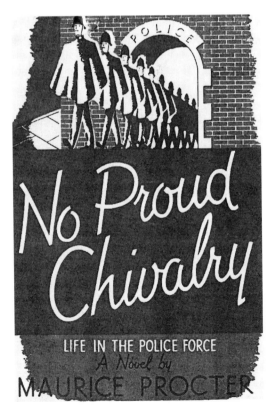

Calling All Cars

HENRY HOLT

Collins Crime Club 1934
artist: **unknown**

'*Calling All Cars,* Calling All Cars': the
insistent message was being broadcast into
the night from Scotland Yard. This fast-
moving tale is typical of Henry Holt, who
wrote over 20 thrillers. It is the eighth
investigation for Detective-Inspector Silver
of Scotland Yard, here searching for an
elusive master criminal, The Shadow, who
constantly hurls taunts at the police: 'This
game could be more amusing if your
funny little flatties showed at least
elementary signs of intelligence.' The
wrapper is red, black and white on blue
and depicts a Flying Squad car speeding
through the night towards the Yard itself,
where Silver's inquiries have led him.
Listening through their earphones, the
policemen know at last that the net is
being closed upon The Shadow.

Murder on Wheels

STUART PALMER

Long n.d. (1932)
artist: **unknown**

Murder on Wheels is the second case of
Hildegarde Withers and opens with a
collision between Laurie Stait's 'open blue
Chrysler' and the 'north-bound yellow
taxi' driven by Al Leech (Hackman's
Badge 4588). Most of the 'rush-hour
traffic on the Avenue' has stopped in
response to Officer Francis X. Doody's
whistle, but the Chrysler has lost its driver
and is 'running wild'. Stait has been
yanked from his car by 'a noose of twisted
hempen rope' round his neck: 'up into the
air, over the rumble seat and down to the
street – backwards!' He now lies on the
pavement, 'sprawled out on his back', his
cigarette still burning on his lapel. Officer
Doody dominates the wrapper.

Policemen in the Precinct

E.C.R. LORAC

Collins Crime Club 1949
artist: **unknown**

Life in the north-midland town of Paulborough is dominated by its ancient Norman abbey. The town is godly on the surface but seethes underneath with gossip, innuendo, suspicion and hatred. The *Policemen in the Precinct* are E.C.R. Lorac's stalwart detectives, Chief-Inspector Robert Macdonald and Detective-Inspector Reeves. They have come to Paulborough to investigate the murder of the worst of the scandalmongers, Mrs Mayden. Macdonald strolls 'leisurely round the sunlit lawns of the precinct, pondering deeply' the fact that 'Once a man has committed murder with impunity, he'll try it again'. A policeman patrolling the abbey precinct at night features on the wrapper.

Crime Wave at Little Cornford

HERBERT ADAMS

Macdonald 1948
artist: **Stein**

There are three main incidents making up the *Crime Wave at Little Cornford*. In this usually peaceful village, someone has damaged the face of the angel on the local war memorial; someone has held up and robbed the guests at Mr Gurzle's party; and someone has used hyoscine to poison wealthy Mrs Prescott. This trio of problems proves too much for Chief-Inspector Goff of New Scotland Yard until Roger Bennion puts him on the right track. Stein's wrapper for this Herbert Adams novel has a design in red, blue, white and black. It shows Police Constable Pollard looking in disgust at the defaced war memorial, the Cornford Angel, its face and hands 'covered … with black paint'.

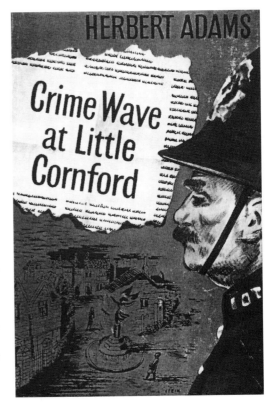

Maigret in Court

GEORGES SIMENON

Hamish Hamilton 1961
artist: **Youngman Carter, after Daumier**

Maigret in Court is one of the many crime novels of Georges Simenon, about 80 of which feature Inspector Jules Maigret, his pipe-smoking detective working from an office at the police headquarters in Paris. Gaston Meurant is on trial for a double murder, but Maigret is convinced of his innocence and must try to convey this to the jury. 'He saw … the figures of the jury … and behind the black gowns of the barristers, the accused man … staring intently at him.' Youngman Carter's brown and white wrapper adopts the style of Daumier for a group of advocates gathered on the steps outside the Palais de Justice in Paris. In the foreground, in black, is Gaston Meurant, the prisoner at the bar.

Verdict of Twelve

RAYMOND POSTGATE

Collins Crime 1940
artist: **unknown**

Verdict of Twelve is the extraordinary first novel of Raymond Postgate, at once an account of a murder trial with particular emphasis on the jury and an exemplary whodunit that reserves the ironic truth of how the victim died until the closing page. The simple design of the scales of justice is especially appropriate, since the fate of the woman in the dock remains truly in the balance until the verdict is pronounced. The novel demonstrates the fallible nature of evidence and shows how the verdict is in part determined by the jurors' personalities and experience. By a particularly bold stroke, one is herself an undetected murderer.

Death on the Borough Council

JOSEPHINE BELL

Longmans, Green 1937
artist: **unknown**

Death on the Borough Council is Josephine Bell's second novel and features her doctor-detective, David Wintringham. PC Evans is on the spot when Councillor Hicks is found dead at the Stepping Public Library. He keeps his head and acquits himself well. The artist gives us an accurate but partial view of the scene: the dead man 'fallen forward on his face, his left arm thrown across his chest'; the table 'a sea of blood' flowing onto the floor to form 'a dark red patch with radiating splash marks all round it'; and 'the knife ... half in and half out of the sticky mess on the table'.

Death Walks in Eastrepps

FRANCIS BEEDING

Hodder & Stoughton 1931
artist: **unknown**

'Francis Beeding' was the pseudonym of John Leslie Palmer and Hilary St George Saunders, who wrote together over 30 crime novels, many of which are thrillers. One murder will bring even the smallest hamlet into the public eye; but in *Death Walks in Eastrepps*, a classic whodunit, five murders are committed in the same brutal way, at the same hour on the same day in successive weeks, so that the village becomes notorious. The wrapper looks as if Stead was the artist and is green and blue on white. It shows Sergeant Ruddock and Constable Birchington 'conducting a house-to-house inquiry in Norwich Road'. Even when the sergeant believes he has his man, a further murder is attempted.

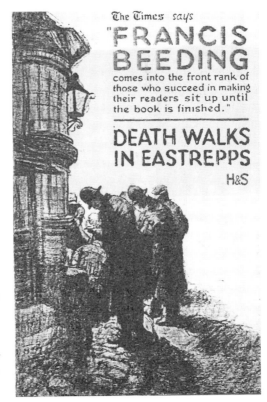

The Seat of the Scornful

JOHN DICKSON CARR

Hamish Hamilton 1942
artist: **unknown**

Mr Justice Ireton dominates the wrapper of John Dickson Carr's *The Seat of the Scornful*, which is red, turquoise and black on white: 'He was a small man, plump rather than fat. Nobody would have guessed … that under his red robe, slashed with black, he was hot and weary at the end of the Westshire spring assizes.' When his daughter Constance has become engaged to Anthony Morrell, the Judge has attempted to pay him to leave her alone. Later, he is discovered 'sitting in an easy chair, some half a dozen feet from' the corpse of Anthony Morrell, 'with a revolver in his hand'. To prove his innocence he enlists the help of Dr Gideon Fell.

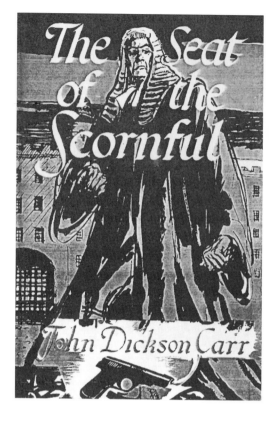

The Case is Closed

PATRICIA WENTWORTH

Hodder & Stoughton 1937
artist: **unknown**

Geoffrey Grey is in prison for the murder of James Everton at the outset of Patricia Wentworth's *The Case is Closed*. Hilary Carew, the cousin of Geoffrey's wife, meets Everton's housekeeper on a train and their conversation prompts Hilary to read the Everton file. Her fiancé, Captain Henry Cunningham, takes the problem to Miss Maud Silver, who comments: 'The Everton Case? Quite so. But it is closed.' The arresting wrapper, blue, grey and white, shows the stern eye of the law looking upon the Everton file, which appears to be a closed book. However, a female hand pushes the file open, grasping a letter which will prove that the case is not closed.

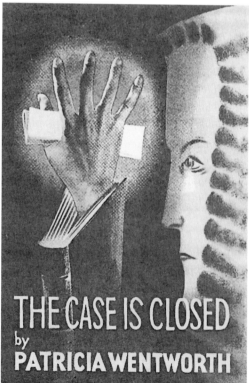

The Groote Park Murder

FREEMAN WILLS CROFTS

Collins 1923
artist: **C. Morse**

The Groote Park Murder starts with the discovery of the dead body of a man in a railway tunnel at Middeldorp in South Africa, close to Groote Park. The first half of this Freeman Wills Crofts novel involves the South African investigation. After the inquiry moves to Scotland, Inspector Ross of the Edinburgh police prepares a confrontation to reveal the truth. C. Morse shows this scene. A figure 'pale and cadaverous was framed in the opening of the door. For a moment there was a breathless silence in the room.' The suspect's 'jaw dropped, his face went greenish white and his eyes started from their sockets, while an expression of deadly horror and fear formed itself on his features.' [See colour section, page (h).]

The Burning Court

JOHN DICKSON CARR

Hamish Hamilton 1937
artist: **Abbey**

The Burning Court shows John Dickson Carr's writing at its best. Miles Despard dies of arsenic poisoning on the evening of the 'masquerade ball at St David's'. He is buried in a sealed crypt, 'under the private chapel, where nine generations of Despards had been set away in tiers, like outworn books'. Though the seal remains unbroken, the body is later found to be missing. On the evening he died Despard was visited by a woman 'in old-fashioned clothes', who 'went out of the room by a door which does not exist'. The case seems to have links with seventeenth-century witchcraft and nineteenth-century murder. Past and present co-exist in Abbey's design, which shows a murder trial before the President of the Tribunal in 1861 and the mask and poison associated with the modern murder. [See colour section, page (h).]

The Cat's Eye

R. AUSTIN FREEMAN

Hodder & Stoughton n.d. (1923)
artist: **Gordon Robinson**

The Cat's Eye opens with a chance encounter for Robert Anstey, KC, leading to his immediate involvement in a murder inquiry. Mr Drayton of Rowan Lodge, Hampstead is found shot in his private museum of antique jewellery and small, 'inscribed objects' with interesting associations. A drawer has been rifled and a cat's-eye pendant, 'set with a single cymophane' and gnomically inscribed, has been stolen. Anstey is a friend of Dr Thorndyke, who is soon at work on the case. Gordon Robinson's striking green wrapper shows the temporary guardian of Rowan Lodge, who confronts them when they arrive: 'a uniformed constable who regarded [them] stolidly and enquired as to [their] business'. [See colour section, page (h).]

The Jury

EDEN PHILLPOTTS

Hutchinson 1927
artist: **unknown**

The Jury at Redchester Assize Court is attending the murder trial of Juanita Heron, of whom, as the book progresses, the personality is convincingly conveyed. Eden Phillpotts allows the reader to share in the thought processes of each of the 12 jurors as they arrive at their verdict. 'Ten men and two women occupied the jury box and their eyes were bent upon the judge's lips.' Mr Bowlby, auctioneer and foreman of the jury, is shown resting his arm on the box and watching proceedings through his monocle. Next to him is Mary McCoy, who runs a stationer's shop: 'fair and still under fifty … in dark plum colour with a boa of black fur round her neck'. Beside her is Mrs Louisa Bartlett, 'a thin and wrinkled dame with … an obstinate mouth and forehead'. [See colour section, page (h).]

11
The Detectives

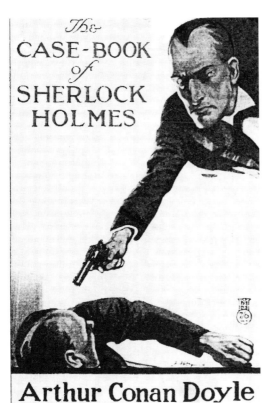

The Case-Book of Sherlock Holmes

ARTHUR CONAN DOYLE

John Murray 1927
artist: **J. Abbey**

Sir Arthur Conan Doyle's *The Case-Book of Sherlock Holmes* contains 12 stories about the world's most famous detective, who runs a consultancy from his rooms at 221B, Baker Street in Marylebone. Abbey's illustration is for 'The Three Garridebs' and shows Holmes aiming a pistol at Killer Evans, who has just emerged from a trapdoor to find Holmes and Watson awaiting him and two pistols 'pointed at his head'. The artist exactly records his 'glare of baffled rage' at the realization. He also shows a striking impression of Holmes, with his piercing eyes set above an aquiline nose. The great detective features in four novels and 56 stories, assembled in five collections, of which this is the last.

The Scandal of Father Brown

G.K. CHESTERTON

Cassell 1935
artist: **Noel Syers**

The Scandal of Father Brown is the last of the five collections featuring G.K. Chesterton's Roman Catholic priest. It contains eight stories in its original form, nine in the Penguin of 1978, where 'The Vampire of the Village' is added. Father Brown, whose cherubic portrait by Noel Syers adorns the first edition wrapper, is among the least conventional of detectives. Though physically 'a drab and insignificant little man', he has powers of perception so far beyond the ordinary that he appears continually at cross-purposes with everyone else: as when Professor Openshaw claims that 'Five men have disappeared' and Father Brown retorts that none has.

Charlie Chan Carries On

EARL DERR BIGGERS

Cassell 1931
artist: **unknown**

Charlie Chan Carries On concerns a series of murders on a world-tour taking in London and Honolulu. Chief-Inspector Duff of Scotland Yard takes care of the London end but Inspector Chan takes over in Honolulu, when Duff is wounded in Chan's own office. He sails with the company on the 'President Arthur'. Chan has six recorded cases between 1925 and 1931, of which this is the fifth. His picturesque aphorisms are a disinctive trademark. The splendid portrait on the wrapper shows him looking thoughtful over a cigar: 'very fat indeed', his 'cheeks … as chubby as a baby's, his skin ivory-tinted, his black hair close-cropped, his amber eyes slanting'.

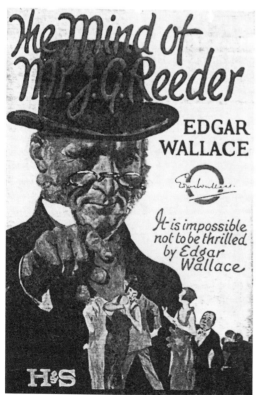

The Mind of Mr. J.G. Reeder

EDGAR WALLACE

Hodder & Stoughton 1925
artist: **unknown**

Edgar Wallace's *The Mind of Mr. J.G. Reeder* is a collection of eight linked stories. The yellow wrapper is dominated by the seemingly benign figure of Reeder, pointing an accusatory finger at a group of well-dressed men and women, who are reacting with shock or despair. Reeder wears the clothes of an old-fashioned gentleman, the effect completed by a derby hat, side whiskers and the steel rimmed pince-nez over which he is gazing. Despite these aids to sight, he is a deadly shot with a revolver. He has an 'extraordinary memory for faces' and a thorough understanding of the criminal mind. He also has an unemotional nature, disliking 'fuss of all kinds': 'There was a quietude and sedateness about the Public Prosecutor's office which completely harmonised with the tastes and inclinations of Mr. J.G. Reeder.'

She Wouldn't Say Who

DELANO AMES

Hodder & Stoughton 1957
artist: **unknown**

She Wouldn't Say Who is the penultimate adventure of Dagobert and Jane Brown, the seated couple on the wrapper. Despite Dagobert's resolute avoidance of regular employment, seven of their cases take place during foreign holidays, one in America, six in Europe. The standing woman is a Viennese actress called Zizi, a 'heavenly creature' with 'glowing, coppery red hair'. She is cast for the leading part in 'How long, O Lord', a play adapted by Dagobert from an unpublished novel by Jane: hence Dagobert's play-script. She also plays the role of the Other Woman in the Browns' marriage: hence Jane's quizzical expression.

Detectives in Gum-Boots

ROGER EAST

Collins Crime Club 1936
artist: **V. Asta**

Asta's white, red and black design for Roger East's *Detectives in Gum-Boots* depicts the husband-and-wife team of Colin and Louie Knowles, who investigate the disappearance of Lord Thurcaston from Rallaton House. An anonymous letter has hinted at his death and his body is subsequently found: 'They are bringing him out now ... out of the ice-house ... he's shot himself!' The mysterious and guilty actions of Lord Thurcaston's wife and son, and even his butler, give Colin and Louie ample scope for their amateur inquiries. Several political personages also stand to gain by his removal. Colin seeks to be a jump ahead, examining the evidence 'before all the police experts had been up to their tricks'.

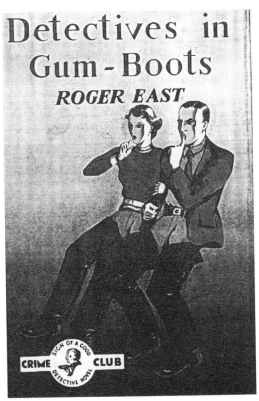

The Puzzle of the Briar Pipe

STUART PALMER

Collins Crime Club 1936
artist: **unknown**

The Puzzle of the Briar Pipe is the sixth case of Hildegarde Withers, 'a prim-looking schoolteacher of uncertain age and certain temperament'. It opens in New York's Central Park, where she is exercising her wire-haired terrier, Dempsey. A 'Code 44' message to a police car draws her to the corpse 'on the bridle path opposite West Eighty-sixth Street': 'Miss Withers' nostrils widened and into her blue eyes … there came the look of a small boy who has just seen the fire engines go past'. The briar pipe, 'warm and pungent-smelling', 'battered and blackened', is rescued by Hildegarde from 'the soft mud which still bore the impress of the dead body'. Its owner is identified on the penultimate page of the narrative.

Miss Hogg and the Brontë Murders

AUSTIN LEE

Cape 1956
artist: **C.W. Bacon**

Miss Hogg and the Brontë Murders is the third of Austin Lee's novels with Flora Hogg as detective. Having retired from teaching on her father's death, Miss Hogg sets up her plate as a private investigator in Acacia Avenue, South Green, where her telephone number, like Scotland Yard's, is 1212. Milly Brown, a children's writer from Tolleshunt D'Arcy, visits her frequently and acts as Watson. C.W. Bacon shows them at Haworth, engaged in the 'formidable climb up a cobbled street which, having veered to the right half way up, becomes steeper and narrower'. Hogg's purple suit confirms her star status: otherwise, the drawing is black and white on pale green.

Cork in Bottle

MACDONALD HASTINGS

Joseph 1953
artist: **Richard Barton**

Cork in Bottle is the second of five genial thrillers featuring Montague Cork, general manager of the Anchor Accident Insurance Co., whose portrait appears in the lower half of Richard Barton's wrapper, which it shares with Stagg Hall, 'a magnificent eighteenth-century mansion' near the Norfolk coast. He resembles 'a kindly old bloodhound ... in a black suit with pin-striped trousers'; and his cases arise when his professional instincts warn him that something is amiss, arousing his curiosity and impelling him to investigate. *Cork in Bottle* is launched by his discovery that the boots he has left outside his door have been borrowed in the night.

My Kingdom for a Hearse

CRAIG RICE

Hammond 1959
artist: **Sax**

My Kingdom for a Hearse is one of the later cases of John J. Malone, the hard-drinking Chicago lawyer of whom Sax presents a neat miniature portrait on the grey wrapper. He is 'an untidy man', 'short, heavy ... with thinning dark hair', 'a red, perspiring face' and a voice 'like a pair of old rusty gates swinging in the wind'. From his first appearance in 1939, all his investigations are shared with Jake and Helene Justus, convivial kindred spirits. Here they encounter Delora Deanne, a cosmetics model who is, in fact, a composite of several women, each with a perfect feature. Her component parts share the wrapper with Malone, who becomes involved when her 'slender, graceful hands' are sent through the post.

The Other Island

E.H. CLEMENTS

Hodder & Stoughton 1956
artist: **unknown**

The Other Island finds Alister Woodhead in
mid-career as a troubleshooter for British
Security. Lanty and St Ninian are adjacent
islands off the south coast of Wales, the
former with a religious community, the
latter with a research station. The blue
wrapper shows Alister 'at the base of
Lanty's sheer cliffs, brooding' and
'motionless, gazing across at the smaller of
the two islands'. He has been searching for
Owen Guirder, a former Nazi supporter
with a 'traitorous past', who has
disappeared from his home on Lanty. As
Alister has anticipated, he is found
drowned soon after.

The Case of the Counterfeit Colonel

CHRISTOPHER BUSH

Macdonald 1952
artist: **unknown**

The Case of the Counterfeit Colonel involves
Ludovic Travers in the murder of what the
blurb delicately calls 'a gentleman of
military aspect'. He is now the owner of
the Broad Street Detective Agency and his
current assignment takes him to the 'house
called Redgates' at Stapley Green. He is
present when the part-time housekeeper
discovers the body of her employer, a
scene vividly rendered by the artist: 'She
was blundering in, uncertain of her steps
… her hand … at her mouth … her eyes
… screwed up in horror'. The portrait of
Ludo is impeccable, even to the 'back lock
of hair that not even glue can flatten'.

She Died Because...

KENNETH HOPKINS

Macdonald 1957
artist: **Stein**

She Died Because... is the first of three
comic crime novels involving Dr William
Blow and Professor Gideon Manciple,
elderly scholars living by the sea, one
above the other, at 10 Priory Place. Stein's
blue wrapper shows them staring grimly at
each other over the body of Mrs Solihull,
Blow's housekeeper, recognized by the
police on their arrival as Flash Elsie. The
fun arises from their courtly other-
worldliness and rambling academic
discourse, both wholly at variance with the
brisk criminous world in which they
suddenly find themselves. Choice
misunderstandings abound: "'I very often
hear her singing through the wall."
"Singing through the wall?" "Through the
wall, singing. Dear me, how pedantic you
policemen are.'"

Heavenly Bodies

THURMAN WARRINER

Hodder & Stoughton 1960
artist: **unknown**

Heavenly Bodies ends the joint recorded
career of Charles Ambo, once
'Tonchester's best-known estate agent and
valuer', and the Venerable Grantius
Fauxlihough Toft, Archdeacon for the
diocese. The former is 'a gentle man, a
scholar' and bibliophile, always 'carefully
dressed', 'badger-like in sober grey and
black'. The latter, by contrast, is 'a glutton
and a wine-bibber', 'a giant of a man with
a vast face and a noble tier of chins, with
legs round and solid as the pillars of Gaza'.
The brown and yellow wrapper shows
them at Old Heddle Church beside the
Archdeacon's car, en route for their
meeting with the Rev. Ross Quinton,
whose wish to resign his living has stirred
them into action.

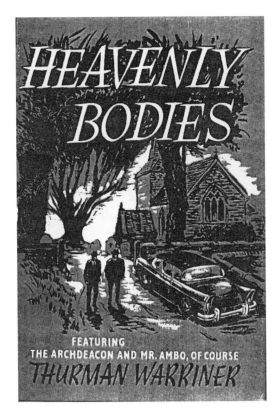

Ill Met by Moonlight

LESLIE FORD

Collins Crime Club 1937
artist: **unknown**

Ill Met by Moonlight is the novel in which
Leslie Ford introduces Grace Latham and
teams her for the first time with Colonel
John Primrose, whose second case this is.
An attractive widow, still under 40, she is
affluent and well-connected, with a house
in Washington, where the Colonel is a
neighbour. She is spending the summer by
Chesapeake Bay when she hears 'the
familiar sound of the murderer's clock' in
Rodman Bishop's library.
Characteristically, she decides to suppress
the evidence and is caught in the act by
the artist, who shows her stowing it 'in the
bottom drawer of the desk under some
papers'.

Death of an Eloquent Man

CHARLOTTE MURRAY RUSSELL

World's Work 1937
artist: **unknown**

Death of an Eloquent Man is the second of
the Jane Amanda Edwards novels by
Charlotte Murray Russell. Miss Edwards is
'forty-odd' and weighs in at 'one hundred
eighty-odd pounds'. She has 'energy and
to spare' and unlimited curiosity: as she
says herself, 'I like to see what I can see'.
Though less well-heeled than formerly, she
belongs to 'one of the best old families in
Rockport', Wisconsin. The 'eloquent
man' of the title is a congressional
candidate of 'the table-pounding school of
oratory', shot dead while leaving
Rockport's Town Hall, after delivering a
speech. The wrapper shows Jane in a
characteristic pose, framed by red curtains,
one of which she is pushing aside.

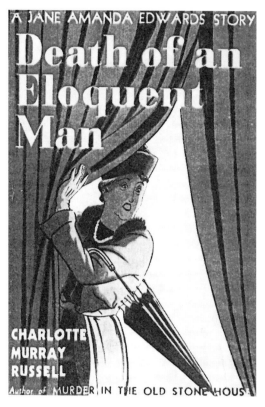

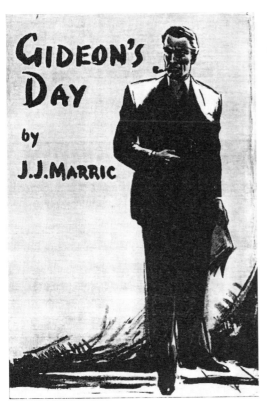

Gideon's Day

J.J. MARRIC

Hodder & Stoughton 1955
artist: **unknown**

Detective-Superintendent George Gideon
of Scotland Yard, later Commander
Gideon, is the creation of John Creasey,
writing under the pseudonym 'J.J. Marric'.
In all, there are 21 Gideon books by
Creasey and *Gideon's Day* is the first. All
are good examples of the British police
procedural novel. In the course of one
long day, Gideon has many types of crime
to deal with, from hit-and-run driving to
drug traffic, from mail-van robbery to
murder. The narrative cleverly interweaves
all these different investigations. At the
start of the series Gideon is 'not yet fifty'.
He stands six feet two and is
'distinguished-looking, with iron-grey hair
… hooked nose … a big, square chin' and
'slatey blue' eyes. The artist portrays him
smoking a pipe against a green
background.

Murder in Crown Passage

MILES BURTON

Collins Crime Club 1937
artist: **unknown**

Murder in Crown Passage is the fifteenth case
of Inspector Arnold, one of the longest-
serving of fictional detectives, with 30
years and nearly 60 cases to his credit. He
first appears in *The Three Crimes* in 1931
and makes his final appearance in *Death
Paints a Picture* in 1960. In most of his cases
he works with Desmond Merrion, a genial
toff with a yen for criminal investigation,
more perceptive and imaginative than
himself. Here they investigate murder at
Faston Bishop, where Mrs Binsted
stumbles over the corpse of her lodger.
Arnold is shown examining the footprints
in Mr Crudwell's garden, which are
'obviously made by a man' and are
'extraordinarily clear' where 'they cross the
cultivated ground'.

The Hollow Chest

ALICE TILTON

Norton 1941
artist: **unknown**

The Hollow Chest is the fifth of the eight
cases of Leonidas Witherall, the retired
schoolmaster and sometime janitor who
inherits the school at which he taught for
40 years, Meredith's Academy in
Daltonville. He resembles Shakespeare –
'so much so that it seemed as if an
engraved frontispiece or library bust had
suddenly come to life'; and he makes a
comfortable living from a popular thriller
series about Lieutenant Haseltine, written
under the pseudonym 'Morgatroyd Jones'.
The wrapper portrait shows him, correctly,
in 'formal evening attire', 'a distinguished
figure in top hat and tails', clutching the
'cumbrous little chest' that causes so much
confusion.

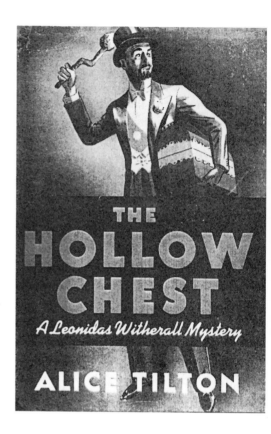

Mr Pinkerton has the Clue

DAVID FROME

Longmans, Green 1936
artist: **Kenneth Inns**

Mr Pinkerton has the Clue features the Evan
Pinkerton of the later novels rather than
the David Pinkerton who first appeared in
1930 in *The Hammersmith Murders*. He has
also undergone a change in status, from
hag-ridden husband to affluent widower,
Mrs Pinkerton having 'passed on to a
better land', leaving him 'the very
considerable sum of £75,000'. On holiday
in Bath, he is at the Blandford House
Hotel when Dame Ellen Crosby is
murdered. Kenneth Inns shows him in the
hotel drawing-room with Dr ffytche
dozing nearby, 'watching the pier glass', in
which is reflected Rosa Margolius, 'her
own eyes fastened in the mirror to the
figures motionless in the deep chairs'.

Clear and Present Danger

BAYNARD KENDRICK

Hale 1959
artist: **unknown**

Clear and Present Danger gives Duncan MacLain his tenth case and, as the title suggests, puts him seriously at risk. He is now married to Sybella Ford, who consulted him in *Blind Man's Bluff*; and he is, for once, his own narrator. MacLain is blind, having 'given his sight for his country in 1917'. Despite 'living in perpetual blackout', he has 'forged' himself 'into almost perfect efficiency'. He can judge a man's height by the length of his stride and has taught himself to shoot accurately at sound: hence the gun he is holding on the wrapper. The dog, Dreist, is another of the powerful weapons at his command.

Crime on her Hands

REX STOUT

Collins Crime Club 1937
artist: **unknown**

Crime on her Hands introduces Theodolinda Bonner, known familiarly as Dol. She recurs in the canon, but this is her chief assignment – and even here she encounters Inspector Cramer. Dol is 'a remarkable young woman' of 'practical, impatient and lonely mind'. She thinks for herself, dislikes men and 'wouldn't accept any man as a boss'. Her father lost his money and killed himself: now, in partnership, she runs a detective agency. She is engaged to detach a rich man's wife from a dubious guru; but the case becomes a murder inquiry when she finds her employer hanging from a tree. The wrapper shows her with 'the little blue-metal Holcomb automatic pistol' she keeps for emergencies.

The Layton Court Mystery

(?)

Herbert Jenkins 1925
artist: **unknown**

The first Anthony Berkeley novel, *The Layton Court Mystery*, was published anonymously. It marks the first appearance of Roger Sheringham, popular novelist and amateur detective, who goes on to feature in nine more novels and eight stories. He is a guest at Layton Court when his host, Victor Stanworth, is found shot in his library. He decides to solve the case. The black and white illustration from the back panel of the dustwrapper is of Roger with Alexander Watson, looking for clues in an ash-pit: 'Roger had straightened up abruptly and was scrutinising with bent brows a grimy piece of paper he held in his hand. The next moment he whistled softly. "Here is something, though!" he exclaimed.'

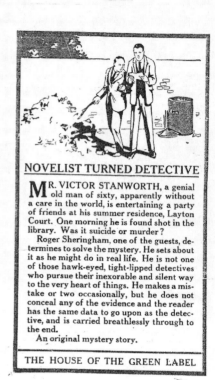

NOVELIST TURNED DETECTIVE

MR. VICTOR STANWORTH, a genial old man of sixty, apparently without a care in the world, is entertaining a party of friends at his summer residence, Layton Court. One morning he is found shot in the library. Was it suicide or murder?

Roger Sheringham, one of the guests, determines to solve the mystery. He sets about it as he might do in real life. He is not one of those hawk-eyed, tight-lipped detectives who pursue their inexorable and silent way to the very heart of things. He makes a mistake or two occasionally, but he does not conceal any of the evidence and the reader has the same data to go upon as the detective, and is carried breathlessly through to the end.

An original mystery story.

THE HOUSE OF THE GREEN LABEL

listen in to Scotland Yard!

The Sea Mystery
FREEMAN WILLS CROFTS

Collins 1928
artist: **H. Dixon**

There are 30 novels and 53 stories featuring Inspector Joseph French of Scotland Yard, the creation of Freeman Wills Crofts. He is one of the major police detectives and is eventually promoted Chief Superintendent. His forte is cracking the apparently cast-iron alibis of many of his suspects. On his debut in 1924, he is described as 'a stout man in tweeds, rather under middle height, with a clean-shaven, good-humoured face and dark blue eyes which, though keen, twinkled'. He has an 'easy-going and leisurely' air, is happily married, likes good food and often discusses his cases with his wife, Emily. For *The Sea Mystery*, Dixon has French looking down on a large crate, washed up on a beach. Inside is the body of a man 'dressed in under-clothes only'.

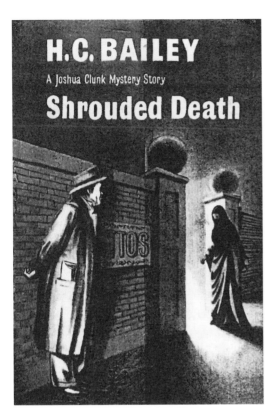

Shrouded Death

H.C. BAILEY

Macdonald 1950
artist: **Stein**

Shrouded Death is the last of H.C. Bailey's novels and a final case for Joshua Clunk, 'the solicitor most eminent in thwarting the police and protecting criminals'. He is an ambiguous figure, subtly and equivocally drawn: in manner a pious humbug, in practice a diligent and infinitely resourceful seeker after truth and justice. No one gets the better of Clunk: he is always ahead of the game. *Shrouded Death* takes him to the Kottos radio factory in North London, outside which Stein shows him waiting and watching. Gliding through the gates is the mysterious 'shrouded woman' who figures so prominently in the investigation. The wrapper is half red, half green.

Case for Mr. Fortune

H.C. BAILEY

Ward, Lock 1932
artist: **? John Campbell**

Case for Mr. Fortune is the eighth Fortune collection, with eight stories, all first published in 'The Windsor Magazine' with John Campbell's illustrations. The wrapper shows Reggie in formal evening dress, looking up from the floor at a pretty woman in lounging pyjamas, probably his wife Joan, but possibly his sister Pamela. Though affecting languor and indolence, Mr Fortune is a master in his sphere, that of medical advisor to Scotland Yard. He is invaluable to the police, acutely perceptive and implacable in the face of evil. He has a bitter wit and displays a fierce, tenacious energy when the occasion demands.

The Adventures of Captain Ivan Koravitch

VICTOR L. WHITECHURCH

Blackwood 1925
artist: **unknown**

The wrapper for Victor L. Whitechurch's *The Adventures of Captain Ivan Koravitch* presents the Captain, dressed in his grey and pink uniform. He is 'late of the Imperial Russian Army', a 'tall, upright, soldierly-looking fellow … with coal-black hair, dark eyes that flashed excitedly at times' and an 'intelligent countenance'. He has evidently taken 'another of the little brown cigarettes' and may at any moment give 'his characteristic twist of the right side of his dark, carefully waxed moustache'. He speaks English 'well and rapidly' and is always ready to tell 'another story', 'One more of what you are pleased to call my adventures'. The 12 recorded stories include some railway mysteries and show the Captain carrying despatches, escaping from an ambush and acting as a judge and a spycatcher.

Poirot Investigates

AGATHA CHRISTIE

Bodley Head 1924
artist: **W. Smithson Broadhead**

The first of Agatha Christie's great detectives is the Belgian, Hercule Poirot, who made his first appearance in 1920. Up to the time of his death in *Curtain*, he appeared in 33 novels and some 50 stories, 11 of which are recorded in the British edition of *Poirot Investigates*. Poirot is a highly efficient private investigator, who uses his 'little grey cells' to great effect. As his friend Captain Hastings ruefully remarks: 'Poirot was right. He always is, confound him!' The black and white wrapper of *Poirot Investigates* has an excellent portrait by W. Smithson Broadhead, complete with egg-shaped head, large waxed moustache, immaculate dress and pointed patent-leather shoes.

Cicely Disappears
A. MONMOUTH PLATTS

John Long 1927
artist: **Ace**

Anthony Berkeley Cox used the pseudonym
'A. Monmouth Platts' once only, for *Cicely
Disappears*, in which Cicely Vernon vanishes
from a house-party after some experiments
in witchcraft. Ace shows an encounter
between another guest, Pauline Mainwaring,
and Stephen Munro, man about town and
detective, here in the guise of a footman.
He swings open the door of Wintringham
Hall and confronts Miss Mainwaring: 'She
had recognised him just as soon as he had
recognised her; there was no doubt of that.
But it was she who recovered first',
frowning angrily and 'handing him the small
suitcase she was carrying'. She addresses him
in 'an imperious and exceedingly cold
voice'. Munro is 'tall, lithe', with an 'athletic
frame' and 'hair inclined to be curly'. He
has a flat in Half Moon Street and employs a
valet, Ebenezer Bridger. [See colour
section, page (i).]

The Mysterious Mr. Quin
AGATHA CHRISTIE

Collins 1930
artist: **unknown**

Agatha Christie's Mr Harley Quin makes
his first appearance on New Year's Eve
during a house party at Royston, standing
'tall and slender' in the doorway and
seeming to Mr. Satterthwaite, who is
watching, 'by some curious effect of the
stained glass above the door, to be dressed
in every colour of the rainbow'. Quin is
the patron of lovers and 'speaks for the
dead, who cannot speak for themselves'.
Mr Satterthwaite, an elderly spectator of
life with intense curiosity about everything,
becomes his emissary and gains the power
to solve mysteries. Quin himself, dancing
and brightly coloured, dominates the
wrapper of *The Mysterious Mr. Quin*, a
collection of 12 of the existing 14 stories
about him. [See colour section, page (i).]

The Solange Stories
F. TENNYSON JESSE

Heinemann 1931
artist: **unknown**

The Solange Stories collects five of the cases
of Solange Fontaine written by F.
Tennyson Jesse for magazines in the 1920s.
Solange is the daughter of a French
scientist and an English lady and makes her
living as a detective. In this capacity, she
depends considerably on 'her own strange
gift, that delicate extra sense … which
warned her of hidden evil'. The wrapper
shows Solange among the grim trappings
of her professional life and matches the
text with precision and elegance. She is
'straight and well-knit as an athletic boy',
with fair hair 'close-cropped in the
courageous modern manner'. 'Hers was
the modern beauty of line … almost
mathematical in its austerity and strict
statement'. [See colour section, page (i).]

Unravelled Knots
BARONESS ORCZY

Hutchinson 1925
artist: **unknown**

Baroness Orczy is noted as the creator of the
first armchair detective, the Old Man in the
Corner, who features in 37 stories, collected
in three volumes. All his cases are narrated
by Polly Burton, a young journalist on 'The
Evening Observer'. Thin, pale, timid-
looking and bespectacled, the old man sits in
a corner of an ABC teashop in Norfolk
Street, off The Strand, consuming milk and
cheesecake and incessantly tying knots in
pieces of string. Mainly by using newspaper
cuttings, he solves cases which have baffled
the police. A head-and-shoulders portrait of
the Old Man in the Corner features on the
wrapper of *Unravelled Knots*, a collection of
13 stories. A 'weird, spook-like creature'
with 'baggy trousers' and 'thin claw-like
hands', he ties 'innumerable and complicated
knots' in a piece of string that entwines
various characters below him. [See colour
section, page (i).]

12
The Clues

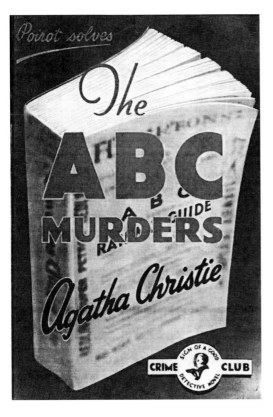

The ABC Murders

AGATHA CHRISTIE

Collins Crime Club 1936
artist: **unknown**

The ABC Murders is vintage Agatha Christie. Hercule Poirot, assisted by Captain Hastings, has to find a murderer who seems a maniac, bent on working his way through a whole alphabet of victims. Beginning with A, he murders a Mrs Ascher at Andover. Proceeding to B, he strangles Betty Barnard on the beach at Bexhill. The wrapper shows the yellow ABC guide to the railways, invariably found near the corpse, open at the name of the place where the murder has occurred. It first appears 'open and turned face downward on the counter' of Mrs Ascher's shop 'as though someone had been looking up the times from Andover'. Later, in Churston, 'An open ABC had been placed face downwards on the dead body'.

Towards Zero

AGATHA CHRISTIE

Collins Crime Club 1944
artist: **J.Z. Atkinson**

Agatha Christie's *Towards Zero* is an investigation for Superintendent Battle and is very cleverly plotted. Lady Tresillian is found at Gull's Point in her 'well-furnished bedroom ... dead – killed – with a great hole in her head and blood everywhere'. In his distinctive style, J.Z. Atkinson illustrates several clues discovered during the inquiry – in blue, yellow and black on white. Depicted are ' a golf club – a heavy niblick', with a 'blood-stained' head and 'one or two white hairs sticking to it'; 'the bell in Lady Tresillian's room with the big bell pull, the tassel of which rested on the pillow near the dead woman's hand'; and a 'small yellow chamois leather glove'.

The Odour of Violets

BAYNARD KENDRICK

Methuen 1941
artist: **G.P. Micklewright**

The Odour of Violets has Duncan MacLain and his dogs working for national security in the run-up to the war and concerned to combat 'sabotage and espionage'. With his developed olfactory sense MacLain recognizes a scent of violets clinging to his instructions from the Intelligence Department; and he comes to believe that such a scent is 'a means of identification, labelling its wearer as a spy' and showing that 'documents ... had been traced, or earmarked ... as originating from agents of the same unfriendly power'.
Micklewright's mauve and orange wrapper shows 'the dead man in the cherry-coloured dressing-gown' in Paul Gerente's apartment and, looming over him, a bottle of 'violet perfume' from 'the House of Bonnee'.

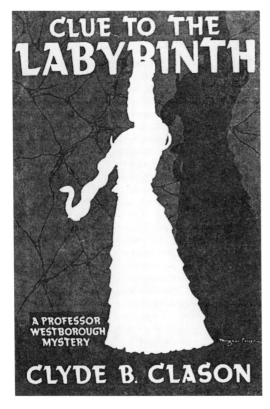

Clue to the Labyrinth

CLYDE B. CLASON

Heinemann 1939
artist: **Youngman Carter**

Clue to the Labyrinth is one of the ten cases of Theocritus Lucius Westborough, a frail, elderly classicist who repeatedly demonstrates a flair for murder investigation. The setting is an island off the coast of California, where Alexis Paphlagloss has erected a magnificent palace modelled on Knossos, with himself in the role of Minos. Westborough is summoned when his most treasured possession is stolen and held to ransom: a priceless chryselephantine statue of 'the Cretan snake-goddess', the 'Lady of the Golden Serpents'. She dominates Youngman Carter's blue-green wrapper, 'a winsomely carved lady, seven inches high – a lady whose ivory features were entwined with tiny golden serpents'.

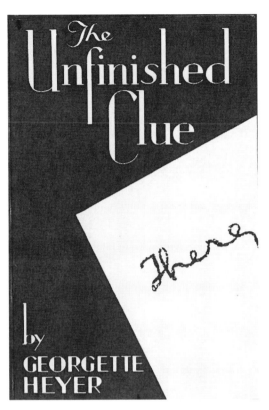

The Unfinished Clue

GEORGETTE HEYER

Longmans, Green 1934
artist: **unknown**

The Unfinished Clue is the third of
Georgette Heyer's 12 detective novels.
General Billington-Smith is far from
pleasant and during a weekend at the
Grange he has given every member of his
household cause to murder him. Someone
does just that, stabbing him in the neck
with a Chinese dagger, below the right
ear. The only clue is that presented on the
black and white wrapper, the 'sheet of
notepaper' found 'under the deceased's
hand … as if he might have written on it
just before he died'. 'Scrawled in pencil' is
the word 'There': 'There was no more;
the faint pencil mark tailed off, as though
the pencil had dropped suddenly from
nerveless fingers.'

These Names Make Clues

E.C.R. LORAC

Collins Crime Club 1937
artist: **Alex Jardine**

'Mr. Graham Coombe and Miss Susan
Coombe invite Chief-Inspector
Macdonald to join in a Treasure Hunt.
Clues of a Literary, Historical and Practical
nature will be provided.' Having 'picked
up the card and studied it', Macdonald
tosses a coin. It comes down heads and he
accepts the invitation. Alex Jardine's design
for E.C.R. Lorac's *These Names Make
Clues* sets elegantly dressed figures round a
table, trying to unravel printed clues.
Graham Coombe, a publisher of detective
stories, stands giving them instructions: all,
save two, 'have had books published by
Coombe'. During the treasure hunt
Andrew Gardien is discovered murdered
in the library and Macdonald's hunt for
really important clues begins.

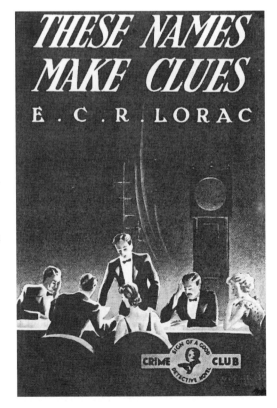

Dancing Death

CHRISTOPHER BUSH

Heinemann 1931
artist: **Nick**

Dancing Death is from the early, baroque phase of Ludovic Travers' career, when Christopher Bush involved him in fantastic events of astonishing complexity and ingenuity. Two members of a sophisticated house-party are found dead after a New Year dance at Little Levington Hall, Mirabel Quest in the house and Denis Fewne in the pagoda in the grounds. The footprints on Nick's wrapper are made by the latter, who flounders home through a heavy snowfall, laying, effectively, 'a deliberate trail – making footmarks that nobody could miss'. The brooding profile of the 'thin, aesthetic face' must also be his: he has much to consider and much to arrange.

Behind That Curtain

EARL DERR BIGGERS

Harrap 1928
artist: **unknown**

Behind That Curtain is set in San Francisco, where the murder of Sir Frederic Bruce is investigated by Charlie Chan. Sir Frederic has been the Head of the CID at Scotland Yard and was famous for his pursuit of 'the essential clue' in his investigations. The artist shows Sergeant Chan considering the significance of just such a clue: the 'velvet slippers embellished with a curious design' that have disappeared from the dead man's feet by the time his body is found. They have an unusual history: but are they truly relevant or are they the 'one essential clue that has no meaning and leads no place at all'?

Dead Man's Effects

H.C. BAILEY

Macdonald n.d. (1945)
artist: **unknown**

Dead Man's Effects is a wartime novel, involving Reggie Fortune with servicemen, enemy agents and international tensions. It begins with hayricks on fire and a drowned landgirl; and its further complications include a burnt male corpse, a contentious air-raid and the 'dead man's effects' depicted on the wrapper. Reggie finds the false teeth 'some twenty yards from the rick in which the corpse was burnt', and they play a significant part in the investigation. He is on the right of the group, thinner and more owlish than in his earlier manifestations. The others, clockwise, are Waldo Rosen, Inspector Underwood, the local inspector, Venn, and the Group Captain.

Death in Seven Volumes

DOUGLAS G. BROWNE

Macdonald 1958
artist: **Stein**

Death in Seven Volumes is the last of Douglas G. Browne's novels and brings to an end the recorded career of Harvey Tuke, the Mephistophelean deputy of the Director of Public Prosecutions. It opens in the London Library, where Inspector Alan Dauncey learns of 'a case of substitution', whereby five books from a set of seven by Mortimer Firebrace 'have been replaced by others from similar … sets'. He is soon investigating the murder of a bookseller who has been advertising for the same seven volumes. Stein's black wrapper shows the pile of seven red books with splashes of blood beneath. Above is Agatha Jackaway, the eccentric daughter of the murdered dealer.

The Lost Mr. Linthwaite

J.S. FLETCHER

Hodder & Stoughton 1920
artist: **Gale**

In J.S. Fletcher's *The Lost Mr. Linthwaite*, retired London solicitor John Linthwaite suddenly goes missing from the Mitre Hotel at Selchester where he has been staying for three days. He is 'a particularly hale and hearty man of sixty-three … well-to-do … not a care in the world … an antiquary of some respect'. Gale's motif combines the two clues that link Linthwaite's disappearance to that 'very lonely spot', Foxglove Lane: the 'grey felt Homburg hat' and the 'gold mounted umbrella' with his initials on it. A diminutive Mr Linthwaite, wearing a grey suit, patent leather shoes and a monocle, peers from behind the umbrella. Foul play is suspected as Inspector Crabbe and Richard Briney, Linthwaite's nephew, make their inquiries.

J.S. FLETCHER
AUTHOR OF 'THE VALLEY OF HEADSTRONG MEN'

The Davidson Case

JOHN RHODE

Bles n.d. (1929)
artist: **Nick**

The Davidson Case is one of Dr Priestley's earlier cases and the wrapper claims it as one of his rare failures. However, it is hardly that, since the narrative ends with a confessional dinner at Westbourne Terrace. Sir Hector Davidson is found dead on arrival at Bratton Grange, stabbed with 'a very efficient stiletto', made from 'a piece of stout steel wire … ground to a fine and very sharp point' and topped with 'a plain wooden ball'. This shares the wrapper with the case that accompanies Sir Hector on his last journey, 'a square box … of wickerwork', 'covered with American cloth' and 'fastened by an iron bar, at the end of which was a formidable padlock'.

8 Faces at 3

CRAIG RICE

Eyre & Spottiswoode 1939
artist: **N.**

8 Faces at 3 is the first of Craig Rice's
ebullient whodunits and marks the first
appearance of the bibulous Chicago
lawyer, John Joseph Malone. It also
introduces Jake Justus to Helene Brand,
who later becomes his wife. They come to
the aid of Holly Inglehart, newly-wed wife
of a bandleader, suspected of murdering
her Aunt Alexandria, 'stabbed three times'
with 'her own Florentine paper cutter'.
Holly has woken 'slowly and unhappily'
from a dream of 'being hanged' to find
herself alone except for her dead aunt,
'frozen' and 'stiff' in her chair. The other
phenomenon that greets her is that shown
on the wrapper: all the clocks in the house
have 'stopped at three o'clock'.

Double for Death

REX STOUT

Collins Crime Club 1940
artist: **Nick**

Double for Death is the first of three novels
featuring Tecumseh Fox, one of several
alternatives to Nero Wolfe with whom
Rex Stout was experimenting between
1937 and 1941. Like most of Stout's
detectives, he is a professional investigator;
unlike Wolfe, he is a slim man, brisk and
busy. Here he investigates the murder of a
financier, who later appears, to identify the
true victim. The yellow gloves on Nick's
black wrapper are found in places
compromising to Fox's client, Nancy
Grant. They are 'of yellow cotton, good
quality, well-made, the kind that women
wear in the summer'; and were 'bought, as
the label shows, at Hartlespoon's', where
Nancy Grant works. They are both,
significantly, for the right hand.

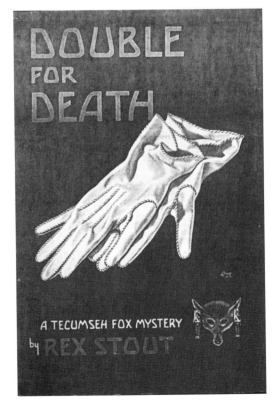

Clouds of Witness

DOROTHY L. SAYERS

Unwin 1926
artist: **J. Abbey**

In Dorothy L. Sayers' second detective novel, *Clouds of Witness*, Lord Peter Wimsey investigates a murder involving his own family. Captain Denis Cathcart, the fiancé of Wimsey's sister, is found shot 'just outside the conservatory door of the Duke of Denver's shooting lodge'. The Duke is Wimsey's brother and is later charged with the murder. J. Abbey illustrates the wrapper with various clues uncovered by Lord Peter: a smoking 'pistol belonging to the Duke ... found near to the scene of the crime'; 'the clear mark of ... a suitcase' 'on the outside of the conservatory'; 'a tiny glittering object ... a diminutive diamond cat with eyes of bright emerald'; and 'the top sheet of the blotting-pad'. [See colour section, page (j).]

Dead Man's Watch

G.D.H. AND M. COLE

Collins Crime Club 1931
artist: **V. Asta**

Dead Man's Watch is a complicated case for Superintendent Wilson, with confusions arising from a corpse of uncertain identity. Is the dead man Harold Bittaford or his brother Percy, or is he, as Mr Fishcote maintains, Henry George? At first the corpse's watch is conspicuous by its absence, but it surfaces eventually to complicate matters still further by appearing to have been stolen and to have had several owners. It is 'a gold hunter watch, old, but of unmistakable quality', with a 'long second hand going right round the face' and a 'stop gadget' at the top. The young woman accompanying it on Asta's fetching wrapper is Dolly Daniells, the fiancée of Ronald Bittaford, who finds the body. [See colour section, page (j).]

Merlin's Furlong

GLADYS MITCHELL

Joseph 1953
artist: **B.G. Yates**

Merlin's Furlong is the 'ancient and dilapidated house' where old Mr Aumbry keeps changing his will to tease his nephews. He is accused of having stolen an Isaurian diptych by Professor Havers, who has in his room 'a large, ridiculous doll' with 'a small imperial' and 'hat-pins ... stuck through various parts of its anatomy'. Yates' black wrapper shows the doll with the diptych behind. It wears, as the text demands, 'plus-fours, a yellow waistcoat, a hacking jacket ... carpet slippers' and 'a check cap'. When both old men are murdered, Mrs Bradley takes a hand; and it is she who establishes the doll's significance, which is other than first appears. [See colour section, page (j).]

The Case of the Flying Ass

CHRISTOPHER BUSH

Cassell 1939
artist: **James E. McConnell**

The Case of the Flying Ass takes Ludovic Travers to France, where he collaborates with an old friend, Inspector Gallois. The affair revolves around the work of Henri Larne, 'a new, tremendous figure in French art', whose paintings are signed with a visual pun on his surname, 'a painted jackass', akin to Whistler's butterfly signature. 'It's ... a flying ass. Its legs are stretched out to give the impression of flight.' Ludo owns a Larne, but he finds the Parisian dealer who wanted to buy it from him, newly dead, with a knife through his ribs. McConnell shows us a corner of a Larne with the ass enlarged by a glass. [See colour section, page (j).]

13
Murder on the Move

Sir John Magill's Last Journey

FREEMAN WILLS CROFTS

Collins Crime Club 1930
artist: **H. Dixon**

Freeman Wills Crofts was a former railway
engineer who worked in Northern
Ireland. In *Sir John Magill's Last Journey*,
the millionaire linen manufacturer
disappears while on a trip to Belfast,
having 'reached Larne … by the Stranraer
boat' and then travelled first-class by boat-
train, stopping off at Whitehead 'to look
up a man on business'. However, a road
on the outskirts of Whitehead shows traces
of blood and a grey felt hat stamped 'J.M.'
is found. Dixon's wrapper depicts the
boat-train, travelling through the night,
with a skull painted on the front. Shown
above the train is the head of a serious-
looking Inspector French, brought in to
conduct the search for Sir John.

Pontifex, Son and Thorndyke

R. AUSTIN FREEMAN

Hodder & Stoughton 1931
artist: **unknown**

Pontifex, Son and Thorndyke concerns the
murder of Sir Edward Hardcastle, whose
solicitor, Mr Brodribb, appears on the
wrapper, puzzling over a confusing letter
bearing Sir Edward's seal. Also featured is
Jasper Grey, shown conveying a dubious
egg-chest to Byles Wharf on his 'two
wheeled truck or hand-cart'. The hansom
could be that driven by Jasper to
Dorchester Square, 'a most shocking old
ramshackle – battered and round-backed
dickey and iron tires – sort of cab that
Queen Elizabeth might have driven about
in'; or Dr Thorndyke's cab to Scotland
Yard, 'as smart and clean as a private
carriage'; or the 'good-sized gig or dog-
cart' that conveyed Sir Edward's body to
Piper's Row.

Plan XVI
DOUGLAS G. BROWNE

Methuen 1934
artist: **B.**

Plan XVI is a boldly imaginative thriller about the 'total disappearance of a 50,000 ton liner carrying upwards of three thousand passengers and crew and a huge treasure'. The story begins in 1919, when Eustace Skyrme and his associates start 'discussing Plan XVI, then in its early stages'. By 1932, when the *Corinthian* 'sailed from Southampton for New York with £3,000,000 in gold bars in her strong-room', they are ready for its execution. Superintendent Thew on land and Bridget Upwey on board the *Cappadocian* share the investigation. B.'s vivid blue wrapper imagines the *Corinthian* being lifted from the ocean by a vast hand.

Too Much of Water
BRUCE HAMILTON

Cresset Press 1958
artist: **H.W.**

Bruce Hamilton was the brother of Patrick Hamilton, famous as the author of the play *Rope*. His miscellaneous output includes five clever crime novels, of which *Too Much of Water* is the last. The Goyax, a cabin ship of the Killick Line, sails from Liverpool to Trinidad, 'with accommodation in a single class for no more than twenty-five passengers'. Three decks are set apart for the use of passengers, the smoke-stack towering above the topmost. Several murders occur during the voyage. H.W.'s design, mauve, red, black and white, captures the fall from the ship of Mr H.O.A. Rottentosser. A fellow passenger, the middle-aged orchestral conductor Edgar Cantrell, finds the logical solution to the deaths.

Death of an Airman

C. ST JOHN SPRIGG

Hutchinson n.d. (1934)
artist: **G.W. Goss**

Death of an Airman is concerned with the Baston Aero Club, of which the flying instructor dies spectacularly, early in the action. The tensions among the members have already begun to emerge when George Furnace plummets to his death in his XT plane with its 'scarlet-and-silver wings'. Goss shows the scene immediately after the crash, with Captain Randall and Arthur Ness, the ground engineer, standing by the burning plane and their dead colleague. Nearby is Valentine Gauntlett's green Alfa-Romeo, borrowed in the emergency by Randall, whose 'golden head' should be visible. En route is Sally Sackbut's 'battered four-seater', tearing 'through a gap in the hedge' and 'down a long steady slope' before coming 'at last … to rest'.

Winged Mystery

ARTHUR W. UPFIELD

John Hamilton 1937
artist: **Stanley Orton Bradshaw**

Stanley Orton Bradshaw has captured the vast expanse of Queensland's cattle station country in his orange and black design for Arthur Upfield's third Inspector Napoleon Bonaparte novel, *Winged Mystery*. The inspector has to discover who stole the aeroplane from Golden Dawn and abandoned it on the floor of a dry lake, leaving an unconscious young woman in the passenger seat. The pilot seems to have vanished into thin air as no tracks can be seen. 'In the centre of the lake … rested a small, low-winged monoplane varnished a bright red … Along the fuselage in white was painted the cipher V-H-U, followed by the registration letters.' Bony is Colonel Spendor's 'worst policeman' but 'best detective': now it is up to him to solve the mystery.

A really first-rate detective story

The Templeton Case
VICTOR L. WHITECHURCH

John Long 1924
artist: **Leslie Stead**

Stead's simple but effective design in purple/grey and white for Victor L. Whitechurch's *The Templeton Case* depicts the yacht *Firefly*, with the prostrate body of Reginald Templeton in the foreground. Templeton is found murdered on his yacht at Marsh Quay: 'The tide was out and the yacht rode at anchor in calm water.' In 'the ordinary saloon of a small yacht … Huddled up on the floor, on his face was the body of Reginald Templeton'. Detective-Sergeant Colson, reputed to be 'an extremely smart fellow', is put in charge of the difficult investigation and uses authentic police procedure to solve the case.

Anything to Declare?
FREEMAN WILLS CROFTS

Hodder & Stoughton 1957
artist: **Jarvis**

Anything to Declare? is the last of the 33 novels written by Freeman Wills Crofts. Peter Edgley and Dick Loxton, lifelong friends, join forces to run two-week cruises up the Rhine aboard the yacht Komforta. The yacht's 'promenade deck stretched forward to the wheelhouse amidships'; in front of this 'came the deck saloon and forward of it a raised sun deck'. Besides their legitimate concern, Edgley and Loxton are in partnership with Bruce Baldwin to smuggle Swiss watches into Britain. Unfortunately, Joseph Rawlins, a passenger, discovers the smuggling and tries blackmail. When he is discovered murdered, Chief-Superintendent French becomes involved. Jarvis' blue wrapper combines the yacht and some of the watches in a lively design with touches of black, white and orange.

Alphabet Hicks

REX STOUT

Collins Crime Club 1942
artist: **unknown**

Alphabet Hicks is the sole full-length case
for Alfred Hicks, an occasional detective
who otherwise appears only in a story. He
is driving a New York taxi when enlisted
by Judith Dundee to prove her innocent
of selling her husband's trade secrets to his
major competitor. The wrapper shows
Heather Gladd and Ross Dundee
advancing towards the 'large black sedan'
in which they suppose Alphabet Hicks to
be awaiting them. It is 'off the road' and
dark, 'but Heather's lights were bright on
the licence plate, JV 28' (which the artist,
perversely, does not show us). More
sensibly, we are not shown, either, the
man 'concealed at the front of the car'
with a 'pistol in his hand'.

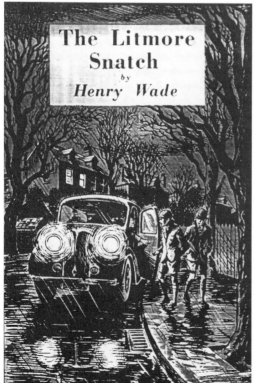

The Litmore Snatch

HENRY WADE

Constable 1957
artist: **unknown**

In Henry Wade's *The Litmore Snatch*, a
campaign against funfairs by a local
newspaper owned by Herbert Litmore
seems linked to the kidnapping of his 12-
year-old son, Ben. The blue, black, white
and yellow wrapper illustrates the
kidnapping, as described by Ben's friend
Jack: 'It was raining a bit when we came
out … In that long avenue – Westway …
– a car came up behind us and a man put
his head out of the window and asked if
we'd like a lift.' Jack describes the car as a
dark saloon, 'Rather grubby … Black or
dark blue'. The book follows the police
investigation to find the driver of the car
and rescue Ben.

Captain Cut-throat

JOHN DICKSON CARR

Harper 1955
artist: **Michael Mitchell**

In 1805, Napoleon Bonaparte waits at Boulogne for the invasion of England. Among his many problems is *Captain Cut-throat*, an unknown who seems invisible, stabbing sentries to death and skewering to their bodies a mocking message signed with his *nom-de-guerre*. For this John Dickson Carr novel, Michael Mitchell shows a red and yellow coach, carrying Ida de Sainte-Elmes, a spy for Joseph Fouché, the Minister of Police, bent on finding Captain Cut-throat: 'Crack! went the whip of the leading postilion … as the coach, built high off the ground with large back wheels and smaller front wheels' and 'drawn by four horses', 'crashed and swayed on creaky springs'.

Sky High

MICHAEL GILBERT

Hodder & Stoughton 1955
artist: **Antony Lake**

Michael Gilbert is a master of story-telling and his thirty-four books are among the most entertaining in the genre of crime fiction. In *Sky High*, country houses are being burgled. Antony Lake shows the burglar making his escape on a motor cycle. His identity is a matter of serious concern to the police and to three amateur detectives, especially when Major MacMorris is killed in an explosion. In a stone outbuilding the police uncover the motor cycle, 'a newish Wolf-Ashton, fast and well cared for'. Its 'most noticeable feature' is 'the double wicker pannier, like a dispatch rider's satchel'. 'Rolled up in a canvas hold-all at the bottom' is 'a housebreaker's kit'.

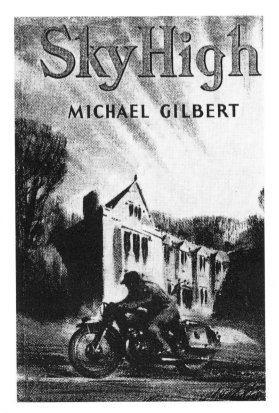

The Loss of the 'Jane Vosper'

FREEMAN WILLS CROFTS

Collins Crime Club 1936
artist: **unknown**

The mainly cream wrapper for Freeman Wills Crofts' *The Loss of the 'Jane Vosper'* shows the sinking of the ship of the title, as viewed through a porthole. The 20-year-old Jane Vosper has been a fine ship of the three-island type: 'a small freight liner of some 2,500 tons register, which worked back and forward between London and Buenos Aires'. 'She had one tall funnel, painted with the company's red and green colours, and her hull was black, relieved only by the white of her boats and upper fittings.' Three explosions cause the Jane Vosper to sink; and when John Sutton, a private detective employed to inquire into doubtful insurance claims, is murdered, Inspector French investigates.

Fatal Venture

FREEMAN WILLS CROFTS

Hodder & Stoughton 1939
artist: **J. Morton-Sale**

John M. Scott is the owner of the 47,000-ton ship, the Hellenique, which cruises as a gambling ship around the British Isles all year and must not sail within three miles of the coast. Because the Government wants to curtail its cruises, Inspector French, incognito, is on board, in case the ship should stray within British territorial waters. When Scott is discovered murdered on a day tour to Northern Ireland, French finds himself with another assignment. Morton-Sale's black, grey and red design for Freeman Wills Crofts' *Fatal Venture* depicts the Hellenique, towering above the flying boat that has come alongside a floating pier, to 'enable passengers to walk direct from plane to ship'.

Beyond Dover

VAL GIELGUD

Hutchinson 1940
artist: **Nick**

Val Gielgud's *Beyond Dover* contains three short novels. The illustration by Nick on the wrapper is for the title story. Nineteen-year-old Sally Martin is shown against an aeroplane, from which passengers and officials are disembarking. Like many people of her generation, Sally has a fascination with air lines, boat trains and trans-continental expresses and she is understandably excited when her boss, Felix Bastin, sends her to Paris: 'It was Sally's first flight … The propeller spun, the chocks were dragged clear – they were off!' However, Bastin is using Sally to sell jewellery he is holding for a client, to pay off his debts: she is being set up as a jewel thief.

Murder at Government House

ELSPETH HUXLEY

Methuen 1937
artist: **unknown**

The wrapper for Elspeth Huxley's first detective novel, *Murder at Government House*, has a panoramic scene in blue, green, brown and white. It depicts the moment when the Miles Hawk aircraft stolen by Sir Bertrand Flower plunges into dense African forest after crashing into a peak. Tollemache and Superintendent Vachell observe the crash from their Percival Vega Gull, which has been chasing the Hawk. 'A spurt of orange flame shot up through the trees … Tollemache dipped the nose of the Gull, straightened out, and circled over the smoking remnants of his machine … of its occupant, nothing remained.' Vachell, the young Canadian head of Chania's CID, has engaged the ace pilot Tollemache to help him track down Flower, who is suspected of murdering the Colonial Governor of Chania.

The Motor Rally Mystery

JOHN RHODE

Collins Crime Club 1933
artist: **unknown (illegible)**

The Motor Rally Mystery is one of Dr Priestley's earlier cases, 'written around the great annual Motor Rally at Torquay', with 'a thousand cars tearing on their thousand-mile journey through the night'. The black wrapper shows the opening scene, as Anthony Lessingham's 'two-seater sports Comet' runs off the road, with Bob Weldon's 'luxurious twenty horse-power Armstrong Siddeley saloon' immediately behind. The Comet has 'apparently swerved to the right', its 'off-front wheel … right in the ditch and the near front … just on the edge of it'. Both its occupants are dead and eventually prove to have been murdered. Bob Weldon's car has Dr Priestley's secretary aboard.

Give a Corpse a Bad Name

ELIZABETH FERRARS

Hodder & Stoughton 1940
artist: **Thompson**

Elizabeth Ferrars has a talent for weaving elegant domestic mysteries and has to her credit 70 crime novels. *Give a Corpse a Bad Name* is the first of these. Thompson's black and white design shows Anna Milne's car coming over a hump-backed bridge on the Purbrook road. She is dazzled by the headlights of a low sports car passing in the opposite direction and runs over the body of a man, whose worn shoe soles are outlined in red by the artist. His face has been 'pulped against the gritty surface'. The corpse appears to be that of a drunken down-and-out from South Africa and is later identified as the son of Sir Joseph Maxwell. Toby Dyke, a suspicious journalist, detects.

Death on the Nile

AGATHA CHRISTIE

Collins Crime Club 1937
artist: **Robin H. Macartney**

A group of travellers, among them
Hercule Poirot, is making a journey down
the Nile, aboard a small steamer, the S.S.
Karnak. Most passengers have cabins on
the promenade deck, the forward part of
which forms a glass-enclosed observation
saloon. Macartney's design for *Death on the
Nile* is mainly brown and blue on white. It
shows the Karnak moored to a bank with,
'a few hundred yards away', 'a great
temple carved out of the face of the rock'.
There are four colossal figures of Rameses,
'one pair on each side of the entrance'.
Murder occurs and Agatha Christie
surpasses herself by weaving a most
intricate puzzle for Poirot to solve.

Kingdom Lost

PATRICIA WENTWORTH

Hodder & Stoughton 1931
artist: **Eugene Hastain**

In Patricia Wentworth's *Kingdom Lost*,
Valentine Ryven has been shipwrecked on
an island when six months old, one of
only two survivors of the ill-fated Avronia.
The other, Edward Bourden, a Fellow of
Trinity, cares for her and brings her up.
He dies when Valentine is twenty and
three months later she is rescued and taken
back to England. Hastain's stylized design
shows a beautiful, radiant Valentine
completely in harmony with her island
environment. Green tresses, like the leaves
of palm trees, flow upwards above red and
white shell earrings. 'The sky was black,
too, but its blackness was all pricked over
with stars.' Valentine's reappearance means
that the Ryven fortune transfers to her
from her cousin Eustace, but then her
identity is challenged.

For the Defence: Dr. Thorndyke
R. AUSTIN FREEMAN

Hodder & Stoughton 1934
artist: **Leslie Stead**

For the Defence: Dr. Thorndyke involves the great detective with the cousins Andrew and Ronald Barton, who are swimming and sunbathing together at Crompton-on-Sea when Ronald's head is shattered by a 'great block of chalk' falling from the cliff. Stead's wrapper depicts the body's arrival at the local police station on a sea-weed cart, a two-wheeled, horse-drawn vehicle with 'a few wisps of sea-wrack that clung to the spokes of the wheel'. The unloading process is witnessed 'with profound interest' by Andrew Barton, who is wearing the clothes of the corpse, since his own have been buried by the fall that killed his cousin. His shadow appears at the foot of Stead's drawing. [See colour section, page (k).]

Murder on the Orient Express
AGATHA CHRISTIE

Collins Crime Club 1934
artist: **unknown**

Hercule Poirot is returning to London from a trip to Syria. On crossing the Bosphorus, he joins the Simplon Orient Express. At first he is accommodated in an upper berth: number seven in the Istanbul–Calais coach; but later he transfers to compartment number one. Despite the efforts of the driver and stoker, shown hard at work on the wrapper of Agatha Christie's *Murder on the Orient Express*, the train is brought to a sudden stop in the night, owing to snowdrifts blocking the line. A Mr Ratchett is discovered dead, stabbed many times, in the compartment next to Poirot. 'Anyone departing … would have left distinct traces in the snow', but since 'there were none', the murderer must still be on the train. [See colour section, page (k).]

Murder at the Pageant
VICTOR L. WHITECHURCH

Collins Crime Club 1930
artist: **Robb**

Victor L. Whitechurch was a clergyman who wrote six detective novels. The *Murder at the Pageant* is shown by Robb in a faithful rendering of the text. Captain Roger Bristow, in his pyjamas, peers 'through the open window' of the sedan chair 'in which Queen Anne was carried on the occasion of her visit to Frimley Manor in 1705'. The 'beam of light from his torch' reveals the seated figure of Jasper Hurst 'in his black velvet cloak, the false moustache and beard torn off his face, and a dark dribble of blood trickling down one cheek from what appeared to be a wound on his temple'. [See colour section, page (k).]

Black Plumes
MARGERY ALLINGHAM

Heinemann 1940
artist: **Youngman Carter**

Art-dealer and picture expert Robert Madrigal runs The Gallery at 39 Sallet Square in London, with 'a history of wealth and prestige behind it unequalled in Europe'. His sister-in-law's fear that 'there's something going on' is confirmed when he is found murdered in a cupboard. Detective-Inspector Brodie makes the inquiries and Mrs Gabrielle Ivory, an authentic Victorian matriarch, arranges the funeral. For Margery Allingham's *Black Plumes* her husband, Youngman Carter, bases his effective design on a yellow street plan of central London, with a red question mark superimposed on Sallet Square. The 'brown-black horses' appear 'complete with silver buckles' and, on their 'nodding heads', 'black plumes … like bunches of gigantic crepe palm-leaves'. [See colour section, page (k).]

14
Murder in the Past

Devil Kinsmere

ROGER FAIRBAIRN

Hamish Hamilton 1934
artist: **N. Matania**

Devil Kinsmere was written by John
Dickson Carr, using the 'Roger Fairbairn'
pseudonym. It is a typically swashbuckling
yarn, with the action taking place at the
court of Charles II in 1670. Roderick
Kinsmere possesses a blue-stoned ring
given to his father by Charles I; it also
happens to be the same as that which
Charles II gives for the identification of his
Messengers. When a King's Messenger is
murdered, there sticks up from 'the back
of his periwig ... the yellow bone handle
of a knife'. Matania's richly coloured
painting shows the King being offered the
knife, while actress Dolly Landis stands by
his side: 'There was handed in ... a bone-
handled knife ... which tapered from its
haft until it was as thin as a sword blade at
the point.'

DEVIL
KINSMERE
by
ROGER FAIRBAIRN

Fear Is the Same

CARTER DICKSON

Heinemann 1956
artist: **Arthur Barbosa**

Barbosa's dramatic wrapper illustration for
Carter Dickson's *Fear Is the Same* has
Georgian figures set against a stormy sky.
The year is 1795 but the young couple,
Jennifer Baird and Philip Clavering, Lord
Glenarvon, have met in another time, in
1955. Jennifer, lovely in pink, watches
anxiously as Glenarvon prepares to face
two adversaries 'Together and at once'.
Colonel Thornton and Samuel Horder are
armed with swords but Philip has only his
fists. The Prince of Wales and the
dramatist Richard Brinsley Sheridan
witness the hard-fought victory after
which Glenarvon comments: 'In all ages,
everything changes. Manners, customs,
speech ... Only fear is the same.'

Death Comes as the End

AGATHA CHRISTIE

Collins Crime Club 1945
artist: **unknown**

'With Nofret had come death' and the theme of death is evident on the orange, grey and blue wrapper for Agatha Christie's *Death Comes as the End*. An Egyptian funeral barge is towed down the Nile. In Renisenb's dream 'She was sailing … in the Barque of the Dead' when 'the prow of the barque, the serpent's head, began to writhe. It was … a cobra' and 'the serpent's face was the face of Nofret'. Nofret is a beautiful girl who has joined the household of the Mortuary Priest, Imhotep, but has a disturbing effect: 'evil matters had festered and raged … then a great stream of evil … had come welling out.' Passion and poison are mixed with devastating effect in this murder mystery set 4000 years ago.

Waltz into Darkness

WILLIAM IRISH

Hutchinson 1948
artist: **unknown**

Cornell Woolrich, writing as 'William Irish', sets *Waltz into Darkness* in turn-of-the-century New Orleans. Louis Durand is unlucky in love, beginning 'the waltz of life' with the beautiful Julia Russell, whose face under its 'tight spun golden curls' holds 'an exquisite beauty he had never before seen'. She makes off with most of his money, breaking his heart and leaving him vowing to kill her. Subsequently, he pursues any blonde who resembles her. The wrapper shows him in evening dress, accosting a voluptuous blonde whom he mistakes for his wife: '"Julia", he panted … Then his hand fumbled under his clothing and he took out the bone handled pistol he'd carried with him.' The waltz into darkness has ended with death.

Scandal at High Chimneys

JOHN DICKSON CARR

Hamish Hamilton 1959
artist: **Biro**

Scandal at High Chimneys is the seventh historical novel by John Dickson Carr. It is set 'during the full tide of Victorianism in the year 1865'. Barrister Clive Strickland is invited to High Chimneys by Victor Damon to advise on the prospective marriage of one of Victor's sisters. During his visit, Matthew Damon, Victor's father, is murdered in his presence, shot between the eyes by an unseen assailant. The scene shown by Biro in black and cream occurs in the conservatory at High Chimneys. Georgette Damon, Matthew's widow, has just admitted to Strickland that she knows who is the murderer. Then 'Somewhere in the con-servatory there was a faint noise': 'holding her, he picked up the lamp'. Someone was listening: 'The murderer's here.'

Fire, Burn!

JOHN DICKSON CARR

Hamish Hamilton 1957
artist: **Philip Gough**

John Dickson Carr's *Fire, Burn!* opens in 1957 with Detective-Superintendent John Cheviot on his way to Scotland Yard in a taxi. Unaccountably, however, he arrives in a horse-drawn cab, finding himself at Great Scotland Yard in 1829. He immediately meets Flora Drayton, whom, later, he escorts to Lady Cork's ball. Philip Gough's elegant wrapper design shows them arriving by coach, the golden-haired Flora in a long yellow coat edged with white fur. Other guests follow them 'up one step, between the dingy pillars' to where 'the door was opened by a footman in orange-and-green livery'. Subsequently Cheviot has to resolve an impossible situation when Margaret Renfrew is shot before his eyes and the only possible suspect is Flora, who is innocent.

15
Creatures in Crime

The Sapphire

A.E.W. MASON

Hodder & Stoughton 1933
artist: **unknown**

The Sapphire is a curiosity among the
novels of A.E.W. Mason in that it both is
and is not a Hanaud story. Hanaud appears
only briefly, visiting with Mr Ricardo a
casino in Savile Row, where certain of the
protagonists are gathered. He inflames the
company by exposing a fraud but makes
no further appearance. The narrative
proper concerns the eponymous jewel,
entrusted by Ma Shwe At to her American
lover, who is intending to abandon her.
She appears on the wrapper, together with
the panther that threatens the life of
Martin Legatt, its eyes 'like huge
emeralds', its tail switching 'slowly from
side to side'.

Mountain Cat

REX STOUT

Collins Crime Club 1940
artist: **unknown**

Mountain Cat is the odd one out among
Rex Stout's crime novels, in that its
protagonist, Delia Brand, does not
reappear elsewhere in the canon. The title
does double duty: for Wynne Cowles, a
'millionaire playgirl known from Honolulu
to Cairo', who might know something
about Charlie Brand's death, and for the
dead cougar, 'fully five feet long',
preserved in Quinby Pellett's taxidermy
workshop, 'its tail curled against its flank
… its left forepaw resting on the carcass of
a fawn'. The splendid animal on the
wrapper is, clearly, neither of these but an
image of the title.

The Hound of Death

AGATHA CHRISTIE

Odhams Press n.d. (1933)
artist: **Demornay**

The Hound of Death contains 12 Agatha Christie stories. Demornay's design is for the title story. In 1921 the Germans entered a Belgian convent and a nun, Sister Marie Angelique, with a reputation for trances and visions, 'called down the lightning to blast the impious Hun – and it blasted him all right'. The ruins of the convent are depicted in blue and white against a green sky. Two walls are 'still left standing and on one of them was a black powder mark that was the exact shape of a great hound'. The peasants are scared of the mark and call it the Hound of Death; shown in green in the foreground of the wrapper. Sister Marie Angelique is now in England. Does she still possess her psychic powers?

The Labours of Hercules

AGATHA CHRISTIE

Collins Crime Club 1947
artist: **unknown**

Hercules was a mythological Greek hero who successfully performed twelve demanding labours and on his death was deified. In emulation, Hercule Poirot decides to take on 12 cases before his retirement, each to resemble one of the 12 labours of his heroic namesake. These are recorded by Agatha Christie in *The Labours of Hercules*. In the opening story a Pekingese dog represents the Nemean Lion: 'according to the legend, Pekingese were lions once'. Pekes are being kidnapped and held to ransom and Poirot is asked to investigate when Shan Tung, the pet of Sir Joseph Hoggin's wife, becomes a victim. The green head of Shan Tung appears on the black wrapper.

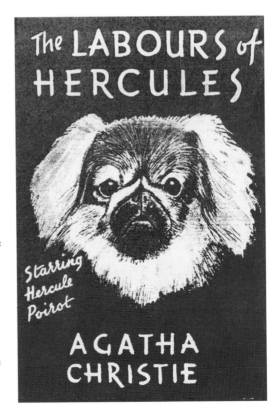

The Man who Shot Birds

MARY FITT

Macdonald 1954
artist: **Broom Lynne**

The Man who Shot Birds collects twelve of
Mary Fitt's crime stories, eight of which
were originally in the 'London Mystery
Magazine'. Superintendent Mallett appears
in eleven stories and Dr Fitzbrown in
seven. The retired lawyer, Mr Pitt, also
features in seven stories, together with his
Siamese cat Georgina, who dominates
Broom Lynne's light brown wrapper. She
is a notably graceful animal, 'pale with
chocolate trimmings': a 'chocolate-and-
cream head', 'chocolate-coloured ears' and
paws, 'slightly squinting blue eyes' and
'variegated whiskers'. She contributes
decisively to all the cases in which she
figures and on one occasion saves 'the life
of a very famous man'.

The Case of the Running Mouse

CHRISTOPHER BUSH

Cassell 1944
artist: **Jack Matthew**

The Case of the Running Mouse is a wartime
case for Ludovic Travers, who has saved
up 14 days' leave and spends them
investigating the disappearance of Georgina
Morbent, at the behest of Peter Worrack.
It becomes a murder case when Worrack
dies suddenly at the West End gaming club
of which he is co-proprietor. Jack
Matthew's blue and brown wrapper shows
him 'slumped back in his chair, mouth
agape', with a soignée blonde woman on
his right. This should be Lulu Mawne,
except that she is a brunette and she has
climbed onto a chair to avoid the running
mouse, which is 'nipping along the
wainscot' and causing 'pandemonium' as
Worrack dies.

The Chinese Goose

HELEN ROBERTSON

Macdonald 1960
artist: **Broom Lynne**

The Chinese Goose is the last of Helen Robertson's four novels and is set on the Thames estuary, near Gravesend, where she lived. Inspector Dynes investigates two sudden deaths and an illegal traffic in swans, which are being sold to gourmet restaurants. Broom Lynne's black wrapper is in his best manner, with its blue-eyed, yellow-beaked bird, perhaps the sole survivor of a raid that leaves 'the long stretch of the mere … stripped of its graceful tenants'. It is as if a 'mortal insult had been offered to nature'. The corpse is one of the gang and arouses less sympathy.

Banbury Bog

PHOEBE ATWOOD TAYLOR

Collins Crime Club 1939
artist: **unknown**

Banbury Bog involves Asey Mayo with Phineas Banbury, the confectionery king, whose peach and cherry tarts are second to none. He acquires Bog House at Weesit on Cape Cod and provides the refreshments for the East Weesit church supper, which prove to have been poisoned. He also quarrels with Abner Grove, who is found dead in the Welcome Wagon 'down by the outermost edge of the bog'. The geese on the wrapper contribute to Janie Banbury's unease at her father's decision to take root in Weesit: 'D' you know what it meant … when geese flew honking overhead and unexpected thunder rent the skies? Well, the Romans … used to run to the nearest cave, and cower.'

Printer's Error

GLADYS MITCHELL

Joseph 1939
artist: **Youngman Carter**

Printer's Error is an early case for Mrs
Bradley, who is represented on Youngman
Carter's blue and brown wrapper by a
sinuous crocodile. Though birdlike in her
earliest manifestation, she is also
continually described as 'saurian', with a
'mirthless grin' that reminds her chauffeur
George – who has 'been to Benares' – of
the crocodiles in the Ganges. Later, Laura
Menzies coins the nickname 'Mrs
Crocodile'. Since *Printer's Error* is pre-
Laura, Mrs Bradley here has the assistance
of her pig-keeping nephew Carey, in a
complicated affair taking in 'bloody ears'
sent through the post and 'a severed hand'
in a printing works. The wrapper also
features the troublesome proofs of 'The
Open-Bellied Mountain'.

Antidote to Venom

FREEMAN WILLS CROFTS

Hodder & Stoughton 1938
artist: **Dorothy Burroughes**

In Freeman Wills Crofts' *Antidote to
Venom*, George Surridge, zoo director,
unlucky gambler and unhappy husband,
needs money to pay his debts and maintain
his mistress in a cottage. His expected
legacy from an aunt has been embezzled
by Capper, her solicitor, and he is driven
to helping Capper to poison his uncle, in
order to regain his money. Surridge selects
for the purpose a venomous Russell viper,
the subject of Dorothy Burroughes'
wrapper drawing, on a green and white
background. This snake is 'rather sluggish
and comparatively easy to handle' and
'with the Pravaz syringe' he is able to
collect 'the drops of venom which in its
rage and fear oozed from the ends of its
poisonous fangs'.

The Case of the Howling Dog

ERLE STANLEY GARDNER

Cassell 1935
artist: **unknown**

Arthur Cartright visits Perry Mason to make his will and file a complaint about his neighbour's noisy dog: 'The dog howls ... mostly at night ... but sometimes during the day. It's driving me crazy.' The dog, Prince, features on the predominantly green wrapper of Erle Stanley Gardner's *The Case of the Howling Dog*. Cartright wants his neighbour, Clinton Foley, arrested, but desires to leave his property to Foley's wife. He fears that the dog's howling means 'there's a death due in the neighbourhood'. Perry Mason and Paul Drake investigate when Mrs Foley disappears and both her husband and Prince, the dog, are found shot dead.

Cork in the Doghouse

MACDONALD HASTINGS

Joseph 1957
artist: **John Hanna**

Cork in the Doghouse involves Mr Cork with Gladys of Hightower, a Staffordshire bull terrier, more familiarly known as Honey. A brindle bitch, she has 'the loins of a runner, the chest and forehead of a wrestler', 'a coalscuttle head', 'a cauliflower ear', a 'pump-handle of a tail' and a permanent grin. She is bequeathed to the Dulcie Davett Dinky Dog Academy, together with the total income from a large estate during her lifetime. Mr Cork takes it upon himself to protect her from those who would prefer her to be dead. John Hanna's raffish portrait of Honey enlivens the bright red wrapper.

The Horseman of Death

ANTHONY WYNNE

Hutchinson n.d. (1927)
artist: **unknown**

Dr Eustace Hailey is called in to certify Lord Templewood insane. His lordship is in fear of 'the horseman whom he hears every night', understandably, since a horseman rides at night to the door of 'the Black Tower' when any member of his family is about to die. He has heard the horseman on the night Orme Malone, the husband of his niece and heir, was killed. The wrapper for Anthony Wynne's *The Horseman of Death* portrays the horseman and his mount in action; it is blue, grey, yellow and green. However, despite the clatter of hooves and 'a loud rapping on the door', there is 'nobody behind the door' when Dr Hailey throws it open.

The Spandau Quid

OLIVER FLEMING

Cecil Palmer 1923
artist: **D. Palmer**

Philip Macdonald's first and second crime novels were written jointly with his father and published under the pseudonym 'Oliver Fleming'. *The Spandau Quid* is the second of these. D. Palmer depicts the hero and heroine of the book, Major Stephen Messenger and his mare, Lizzie, together leaping the Cullrellick and Moorchester railway line. Lizzie 'stood one inch and a half over sixteen hands; black as velvet, shining sleek as silk … Her eyes, tender with a soft-brown blueness, turned on you a gaze of gentleness, intelligence and courage'. It is with Lizzie's help that, while stag hunting, Messenger saves the life of author Henry Bellingham. This leads him into an adventure involving smuggling, hidden caves, gold, conspirators, underground passages, a German U-boat and kidnapping.

The Penguin Pool Murder

STUART PALMER

John Long n.d. (1932)
artist: **unknown**

The Penguin Pool Murder is the novel that
begins with a body in a penguin tank at
the New York Aquarium and ends with
Hildegarde Withers' and Oscar Piper's mad
dash to City Hall for a marriage licence.
Miss Withers is on hand when Gerald
Lester's body is found moving 'in the
circulating current' of 'the last tank in the
line'. She is escorting a 'little group of
third grade pupils' from Jefferson School,
one of whom lingers to watch the 'little
black penguins' 'dashing madly around …
now and then leaping out of the water to
squawk and snap their pointed bills'. The
body accounts for their 'frightened
squawking' and their attempts to 'scramble
madly up the steep side of the tank'.

The Owl in the Cellar

MARGARET SCHERF

Nimmo n.d. (1947)
artist: **unknown**

The Owl in the Cellar is the fourth of
Margaret Scherf's engaging mysteries and
marks the first appearance of her New
York police detective, Lieutenant Ryan.
He is called to Staten Island when Charlie
Murphy finds a body in the cellar of his
family home. The dead man is suspended
from the window 'by his feet, like a fresh-
killed chicken' and appears on the brown
wrapper as a flattened blue silhouette.
Looking on is Eggface, the other occupant
of the Murphys' cellar, whose 'mournful
… slow' nocturnal hooting has threatened
to 'scare the liver out of' Charlie's mother.
The bird has 'a mind of his own' and is
capable of delivering 'a nice rip with his
beak'.

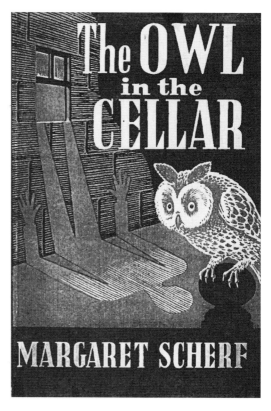

Murder on Leave

G.V. GALWEY

Bodley Head 1946
artist: **Luxton**

Murder on Leave is the first of G.V. Galwey's three novels, all with Inspector 'Daddy' Bourne as detective. It is still wartime and most of the people involved have helped to fight the war in one way or another. The victim is Gruach MacGregor, a VAD, found stabbed 'at the foot of a railway embankment in the Pass of Drumochter' in Scotland. Her body is 'found by a shepherd's dog, whose obstinate barking brought his master'. In the palm of her hand is 'a first-class return ticket from Inverness to London'. Luxton shows the scene in graphic detail, black on orange, with the dog given due prominence.

The Last Express

BAYNARD KENDRICK

Methuen 1938
artist: **G.P. Micklewright**

The Last Express introduces Captain Duncan Maclain, a blind detective trained to shoot by sound. He is consulted by the sister of a District Attorney, who later dies when a Mills bomb explodes in his car. The sole clue is the dead man's final utterance: 'See Beach Subway – the last express'. Micklewright's vivid orange wrapper shows Maclain and one of his German shepherd dogs, with the last express beneath. Since he clearly means business, the dog is more probably Dreist, 'the best police dog in the world', 'trained to be dangerous as a loaded gun', with the 'broad, strong jaws and fore-chest' of a 'runner and fighter'. Maclain's other dog is Dreist's gentle, female counterpart, the seeing-eye dog, Schnucke.

Dead Cert

DICK FRANCIS

Joseph 1962
artist: **Trevor Denning**

Dead Cert is the first of Dick Francis' long series of popular horse-racing crime novels. Trevor Denning admirably records the disastrous fall of the chestnut, Admiral, ridden by Bill Davidson, four fences from home on the Maidenhead racecourse: his wrapper is brown, orange, purple and black on white. Davidson has been 'about to win his ninety-seventh steeplechase', with Admiral 'amply proving he was still the best hunter chaser in the kingdom'; but instead there is 'the flurry of chestnut legs threshing the air as the horse pitched over in a somersault', with 'Bill's bright-clad figure hurtling head downwards' to his death. Alan York, his closest friend, is riding the horse behind and notices that the fence has been wired. After Davidson's death, York determines to bring to justice the men who wired that fence.

The Iron Spiders

BAYNARD KENDRICK

Methuen 1938
artist: **G.P. Micklewright**

The Iron Spiders precedes the arrival of Duncan MacLain and features as detective Miles Standish Rice, 'Deputy Game and Fresh Water Fish Commissioner' for Florida and 'Special Deputy Sheriff for Monroe County'. It is set on Broken Heart Key in the Gulf of Mexico, where Aaron Tuckerton maintains an estate with its own power plant. He is rich, semi-paralysed and 'always in danger' from attempts on his life. When he dies suddenly it is established that he has been 'bitten by a spider: a very venomous spider known as the Black Widow'. Micklewright's powerful wrapper shows the Black Widow – or *Latrodectus mactans* – 'black and shiny, with a globular body' enclosing an angry yellow face, most probably that of the victim.

The Black Camel

EARL DERR BIGGERS

Bobbs Merrill 1929
artist: **unknown**

The Black Camel is set on Charlie Chan's
home ground of Honolulu, where Shelah
Fane, a celebrated film actress, is murdered
while visiting Hawaii. On the point of
revealing what she knows about the
murder of Denny Mayo in Los Angeles
three years earlier, she is terminally
silenced before she can do so. The black
camel, so strikingly shown on the wrapper,
is, in fact, a metaphor for death, preserved
in an 'old Eastern saying' quoted by Chan:
'Death is the black camel that kneels unbid
at every gate'. On the night of Shelah
Fane's death it 'has knelt at plenty famous
gate'.

The Chinese Parrot

EARL DERR BIGGERS

Harrap 1927
artist: **unknown**

The Chinese Parrot takes Charlie Chan to
P.J. Madden's ranch in the California
desert, as guard for the Phillimore pearls.
He assumes the role of Ah Kim, the cook,
a 'plump little Chinese servant with worn
trousers and velvet slippers and a loose
jacket of Canton crepe'. The artist shows
him with Tony, the parrot, a 'little grey
Australian bird' that dies for talking out of
turn: his repertoire includes a 'hideous
cry': 'Help! Help! Murder! Put down that
gun.' Madden attributes this to the bar-
room phase of the bird's history, but Chan
resolves, none the less, to find out 'Who
uttered the cry that was heard and echoed
by Tony, the Chinese parrot?'

Gownsman's Gallows
KATHARINE FARRER

Hodder & Stoughton 1957
artist: **unknown**

Gownsman's Gallows is the last of the three
cases of Richard Ringwood, a young
police detective who trains his own
bloodhound, the eager, slobbering Ranter,
shown on the wrapper with the spires and
towers of Oxford behind her, together
with the body lying by the elms near the
churchyard in Priory Road, where once
'the University gibbet stood'. The dog's
triumph is to trace the corpse to where he
was killed as opposed to where he was
found: 'Ranter stopped, cast round for a
minute and then, planting her forelegs like
columns ... and settling herself firmly, she
lifted her muzzle and gave her voice full
freedom'. [See colour section, page (e).]

Pearls before Swine
MARGERY ALLINGHAM

Doubleday Crime Club 1945
artist: **Vera Bock**

Pearls before Swine is the American version
of *Coroner's Pidgin*, notable for its variant
final sentence and Vera Bock's exuberant
wrapper for the first edition. The book is
set in wartime London, with Albert
Campion on leave and heading for home.
Despite an unknown female corpse on his
bed, he resists involvement but yields
under pressure. A complex inquiry leads
him to fear that the charismatic Marquess
of Carados may also be a traitor, since all
trails appear to lead to him. Campion's
man, Lugg, in 'Heavy Rescue', keeps a
sow in Carados Square, where she
punctuates his doting monologues with 'a
series of acquiescing snorts'. [See colour
section, page (e).]

16
Scent of Death

Monkshood

EDEN PHILLPOTTS

Methuen 1939
artist: **C.W. Bacon**

C.W. Bacon has created a most intricate design for Eden Phillpotts' *Monkshood*. The vivid blue monkshood flowers dominate the foreground with, behind, the graveyard and bay at Coombe depicted in pale green on white. In the graveyard 'Extravagant creations brood amid the humble graves'. There are ships' figureheads, marking the graves of drowned seamen. As a baby, Emilio Campi, the chef at Coombe's largest hotel, was washed ashore in a barrel from a sinking ship. Now he, too, 'lies under the old figure-head of the "Sirena"', one among several of the community to meet with a mysterious death. The poisonous monkshood, 'native' to Coombe, is described as a 'vile herb' that should not be allowed 'to threaten human happiness any more'.

The Red Box

REX STOUT

Cassell 1937
artist: **Eric Fraser**

The Red Box is the fourth of Rex Stout's novels and takes Nero Wolfe on a rare 'mad sortie to Fifty-second Street', to investigate *in situ* the poisoning of a model at a fashion house. Later, Boyden McNair, the head of the firm, dies suddenly in Wolfe's office in the course of a confessional. McNair's 'red leather box and its contents' are bequeathed to Wolfe, 'to be used by him at his will and his discretion', but whatever its significance the box proves elusive and its appearance is long delayed. Eric Fraser's wrapper shows the box with its ornate brass fittings, together with a spotted orchid from Wolfe's plant rooms, in full, curving bloom.

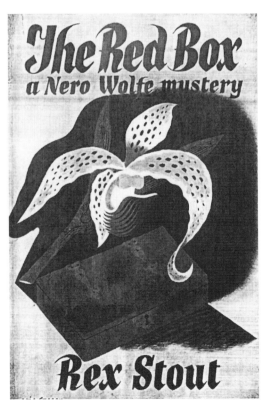

Jack on the Gallows Tree

LEO BRUCE

Peter Davies 1960
artist: **Biro**

Jack on the Gallows Tree is vintage Leo Bruce from his middle, Peter Davies period. Carolus Deene goes to Buddington to recuperate after illness, only to find that two women, each unknown to the other, have 'been murdered during a single night' in the town. Miss Carew and Mrs Westmacott have both been strangled and each is discovered 'laid out as though for burial' and 'holding a Madonna lily'. When a third bloom is stolen from Mrs Gosport's garden, a further death seems to threaten, unless Carolus can prevent it. Biro's wrapper displays two of the 'waxy white flowers' that add such a 'macabre touch' to the affair.

The Moonflower

BEVERLEY NICHOLS

Hutchinson 1955
artist: **G.W. Anderson**

The Moonflower of Beverley Nichols' second detective novel dominates G.W. Anderson's design. Brought from Uruguay as a very expensive seed, this giant convolvulus is one of six growing in rich Mrs Faversham's conservatory, where she is found strangled. It is appropriate that the crime is solved by the endearing Horatio Green, retired private investigator and passionate gardener. 'The moonflower called to him ... it was of incredible beauty. There were three eight-petalled blooms, each of them over nine inches across. They had not only the colour but the quality of snow.' After the murder is discovered, Mr Green has a feeling that the exotic plant 'formed an essential part in the design of a drama that was eluding him'.

Deadly Nightshade

ELIZABETH DALY

Hammond 1948
artist: **unknown**

Deadly Nightshade is the second case of Henry Gamadge, known as the 'bibliophile-detective' from his expertise in inks and founts and watermarks. He is summoned to Ford's Centre, Maine by State Detective Mitchell, who laconically sums up the problem: 'Some children got hold of some poison berries ... Two ... got well, one died, one's missing.' The black wrapper, in series format, features the cause of the trouble, a spray of Solanum Nigrum Linnaeus, with its 'big, black, shiny berries'. It also has a caravan from the local gypsy camp and a female protagonist, perhaps Adele Bartram, with the 'petrified-looking ridges on either side' of her face.

Fish and Company

RALPH ARNOLD

Heinemann 1951
artist: **C.W. Bacon**

Fish and Company is the first of Ralph Arnold's three detective novels, all elegantly composed in the cerebral tradition. Mr Puckle is summoned from his Surrey market garden to Lake Como, where, at the Villa Straven, Lady Malmayes' birthday has, for once, failed to coincide with the flowering of her favourite plant, which is, on the contrary, 'all brown and withered and as dead as a doornail'. When the lady also succumbs to poison, Mr Puckle turns detective. C.W. Bacon shows the hand of the plant saboteur in the act of scattering sodium chlorate over the Datura Stravensis.

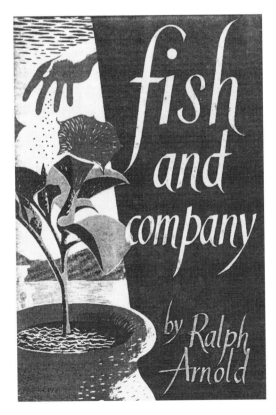

Common or Garden Crime

SHEILA PIM

Hodder & Stoughton 1945
artist: **unknown**

Common or Garden Crime is a horticultural detective novel set among Irish gentry and their gardens. It features Inspector Lancey, who recurs as a superintendent in Sheila Pim's fourth and last crime novel, *A Brush with Death*. Lady Madeleine Osmund dies suddenly, having been poisoned by 'a small quantity of grated root of Aconitum', mixed with the 'raw grated horseradish round the beef' of her last meal. The wrapper is a curiosity, in that it depicts a yellow flower, where the text specifies 'dark blue-flowered spikes' for Aconitum ferox, the cause of all the trouble. Perhaps, like Miss FitzEustace, the artist 'thought … that aconites were those little yellow things', classified by Linnaeus Bex as 'Eranthis'.

The Merry Hippo

ELSPETH HUXLEY

Chatto & Windus 1963
artist: **Rosemary Grimble**

The Merry Hippo is the last of Elspeth Huxley's African mysteries, published 25 years after her earlier series with Superintendent Vachell. A Royal Commission visits the Protectorate of Hapana to advise on constitutional arrangements for its independence. When Lord Bagpuse, the commission's vice-chairman, dies suddenly, it appears that he has been poisoned by mistake for the chairman. Africa is full of poisons, all instantly to hand: 'The wonder was that anyone stayed alive in this country'. Rosemary Grimble's pale green wrapper shows the red 'seed of the creeper Abrus precatorius, found all over the momombo bush and containing a toxin called abrin that could kill a man in twenty minutes'.

No Grave for a Lady

JOHN AND EMERY BONETT

Joseph 1960
artist: **H. Bridgeman Grimley**

No Grave for a Lady is the third of the
Bonetts' novels and the last with Professor
Mandrake as detective. The setting is
Lyonesse, a holiday island where the
German film actress, Lotte Liselotte, is
found drowned. A celebrated 'femme
fatale', she has become a focus for much
intemperate emotion among the holiday
community. Grimley shows her in the
'huge white sun-glasses' that serve as her
'defence' against the curious. The
magnolia is left at her table as a tribute,
'one perfect waxen bloom', 'milky-white
and as large as a small plate': but by the
time she takes her place for dinner it is
'crushed and turning brown'.

A Trail of Blood

JEREMY POTTER

Constable 1970
artist: **Jenny Pocknell**

A Trail of Blood is the first of Jeremy
Potter's historical crime novels and deals
anew with the fate of the Princes in the
Tower. The author pays tribute in a
preliminary note to the 'inspiration' of
Josephine Tey's *The Daughter of Time* and
claims for his 'version of events' that 'it is
as plausible' as that of 'three earlier
practitioners of the art of crime fiction: H.
Tudor, T. More and W. Shakespeare'.
Jenny Pocknell's wrapper places Brother
Thomas of Croyland Abbey against a pale
orange sky, with, prominent in the
foreground, the White Rose of Yorkshire,
running with blood.

17
Pastimes in Purgatory

The Amazing Test Match Crime

ADRIAN ALINGTON

Chatto & Windus 1939
artist: **unknown**

The Amazing Test Match Crime is the latter of Adrian Alington's comic crime novels, each with 'Steady-as-a-Rock' Posse as detective. It concerns a plot to use the English obsession with cricket to bring down the British Empire. Together, a sinister foreign professor, an American 'gangster of the lowest type' and a renegade ex-public schoolboy scheme to wreck the forthcoming Test Match. On the wrapper Sawn-off Carlo, 'a round soft hat on his head', mimes a hold-up with his right hand. His target, one of the 'photographs of old cricketers' in the Oval pavilion, hangs askew and looks glum.

Alibi Innings

BARBARA WORSLEY-GOUGH

Joseph 1954
artist: **Freda Nichols**

Alibi Innings is the first of only two detective novels by Barbara Worsley-Gough, both featuring Aloysius Kelly, an exuberant Irish journalist 'in his late forties', resident in Soho. He has driven down to Alcocks for 'the annual cricket match between the Squire's eleven and the village side' and also, less predictably, for the murder of the Squire's wife, 'bashed on the head' in her study in the course of the match. She has been so widely disliked that motives abound; and in such a context an innings might well, as the title neatly suggests, provide an alibi. Freda Nichols' green wrapper shows a moment from the match, with a noose suspended over the batsman facing the bowling.

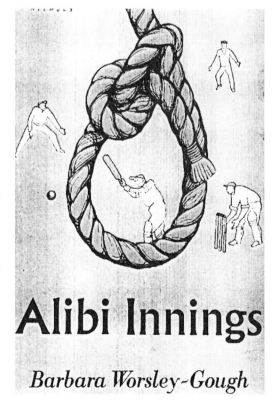

A Pall for a Painter

E.C.R. LORAC

Collins Crime Club 1936
artist: **unknown**

Richard Carling visits Manette's art school, where he was once a student. He notices that Manette's 'still kept up the tradition of fine draughtsmanship', though 'modernism was allowed in the broad flat treatment of masses, in the rhythmical force which bound the composition into a living pattern'. Carling is reunited with Roger Laird, now the teacher of the Life class. It is Laird who figures on the wrapper of E.C.R. Lorac's *A Pall for a Painter*: redheaded, bearded in his painter's coat and with a brush and palette in hand. Behind him is the immense armless Venus under which his dead body is found: 'Lying prone under the wreck of the Venus was a man's body.' Inspector Macdonald's inquiries inevitably centre on Manette's artistic community.

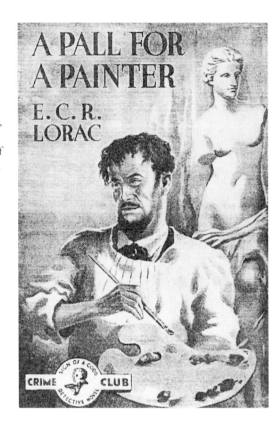

When the Wind Blows

CYRIL HARE

Faber 1949
artist: **Victor Reinganum**

Francis Pettigrew is the treasurer of the Markshire Orchestral Society and his wife, Eleanor, has established herself 'among the second violins'. During a concert, the soloist in Mendelssohn's Violin Concerto is found dead in the soloists' room. Reinganum's striking composition, in brown, yellow, fawn and black, shows 'the huddled form of Lucy Carless' in a yellow dress, together with her violin 'in its open case'. The 'cause of death' is 'evidently strangulation'. As the title of Cyril Hare's novel suggests, the crime and its detection in *When the Wind Blows* involve the woodwind section of the orchestra. When the body is discovered an unidentifiable clarinet player is found to have disappeared. Pettigrew, a former barrister, uncovers the truth.

The Echoing Strangers

GLADYS MITCHELL

Joseph 1952
artist: **Barbara Bradley**

The Echoing Strangers is a rich and subtle story set partly in Norfolk and partly in Hampshire. Each county has its corpse, the former located by Mrs Bradley in the River Burwater, the latter 'struck down with his own cricket bat' during the Mede cricket week. Each also has its handsome twin youth, separated from his brother since childhood but now reunited. Barbara Bradley's apple-green wrapper displays considerable artistic licence, since the blackmailing captain of the Bruke team is not found dead at the wicket but 'lying sprawled along the line of the showers' in the Mede pavilion, 'his head … on one of the drains'.

Death before Wicket

NANCY SPAIN

Hutchinson n.d. (1946)
artist: **unknown**

Death before Wicket features Johnny and Natasha DuVivien before their meeting with Miriam Birdseye, by whom they are supplanted as Nancy Spain's work progresses (though, with a new husband, Natasha survives to *Not Wanted on Voyage*, the penultimate title in the series). Murder occurs at the Fathers' Match at St Ann Athaway's School, where Johnny is to play against a team of girl cricketers. Despite the green wrapper, with its golden stumps, their bails sent flying by a skull in lieu of the usual ball, the match has not even started when one of the umpires fails to come round after a faint, her life going out 'in suffocation and a slow convulsion; in rigidity, and, above all, in a bitter, bitter smell of almonds'.

Hazard Chase

JEREMY POTTER

Constable 1964
artist: **Peter Barrett**

Hazard Chase is set in the world of real tennis, 'the king of games and the game of kings'. The court at High Cheney is formally re-opened with an exhibition match, of which the loser is found dead in the small hours. A former world champion known as 'Old Nick', he lies 'spread-eagled on the floor' of the court, dressed 'all in white', his head 'half-hidden by an arm'. Nearby is a row of eight bottles supporting lettered tennis-balls, spelling out the phrase 'Dead Nick'. Peter Barrett's purple wrapper shows the dead man beneath a large black racquet but disregards the mocking message.

The Nineteenth Hole Mystery

HERBERT ADAMS

Collins Crime Club 1939
artist: **unknown**

The wrapper for Herbert Adams' *The Nineteenth Hole Mystery* shows a dramatic scene in the bar at Allingham golf course in Dorset, where two men meet their deaths. 'On the floor of the ingled enclosure, in a pathetic, almost ludicrous heap, lay the body of the steward.' He lies 'at the very foot of the place where Hugh Denton had been found the week before', but unlike Denton he has not been shot: 'By his side was a heavy iron poker.' Roger Bennion has been looking forward to a week's golfing holiday but now finds himself having to unravel the mystery of two violent deaths. He examines the steward, feeling 'his wrist and his heart': '"Not dead", he said, "but pretty far gone."' Korwood, a fellow golfer, looks on aghast.

James Tarrant, Adventurer

FREEMAN WILLS CROFTS

Hodder & Stoughton 1941
artist: **unknown**

James Tarrant is an unscrupulous self-made man, manufacturing and marketing patent medicines. At the start of Freeman Wills Crofts' *James Tarrant, Adventurer*, he is an assistant chemist. Having recruited Merle Weir and Peter Temple to assist him in building up his business, he betrays them both, causing Merle to exclaim 'I will kill him!'. With his profits, Tarrant acquires The Gables, 'a pleasant little cottage' of which 'the grounds slope down to the water's edge' and the ownership 'includes the fishing rights' over 'a typical trout stream with deepish pools separated by strong reaches'. The wrapper has Tarrant fishing in silhouette, posed against an orange background. When his body is found in the river, Inspector French takes up the case.

Death at the Strike

COLIN WILLOCK

Heinemann 1957
artist: **Denys Watkins-Pitchford**

Death at the Strike is the second of the three 'adventure-thrillers' by Colin Willock, famous for his contribution to wildlife television. All three involve Nathaniel Ironsides Goss, the General Manager of National Periodicals Ltd, whose occasional yen for adventure takes him here on an eventful angling holiday at the Stark Ford Hotel near Caistor, where he hooks 'a big one' that moves 'in a most peculiar fashion' and raises from the water 'something that looked more like an upraised human arm than the tail of a fish'. The moment is recorded by his star photographer, whose print confirms that a drowning man was indeed on the wet end of the line; and Denys Watkins-Pitchford's blue and black wrapper also faithfully records the scene.

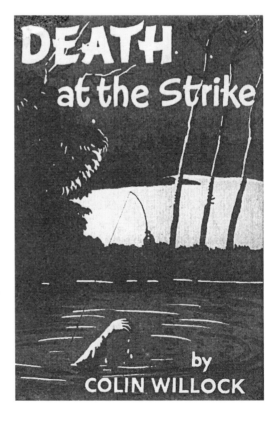

Opening Night

NGAIO MARSH

Collins Crime Club 1951
artist: **unknown**

A new play is under rehearsal at the Vulcan Theatre in London. The company's leading lady, Helena Hamilton, has a new dresser, an out-of-work actress named Martyn Tarne. On *Opening Night*, Martyn has to stand in for another actress, Gay Gainsford, who has had a breakdown. The wrapper shows the first night audience arriving at the Vulcan, 'a new theatre, fashioned from the shell of an old one', with a foyer 'of geranium-red leather, chromium steel and double glass walls housing cacti'. At the end of the performance, Helena's husband is found gassed in his dressing-room. Scotland Yard sends Chief-Inspector Alleyn to investigate his 16th case, as chronicled by Ngaio Marsh.

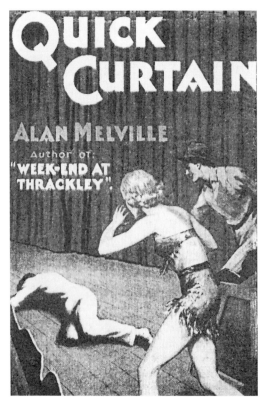

Quick Curtain

ALAN MELVILLE

Skeffington 1934
artist: **W.J. Roberts**

Quick Curtain is one of six lively crime novels written by Alan Melville early in his career, before his success in the theatre. The action arises from a musical comedy called 'Blue Music', which comes to an abrupt end during its first night, at the point where Philippo shoots Jack for kissing his lover, Coletta. When Brandon Baker, as Jack, falls to the ground, there is a 'peculiar dark mark on the stage just where [he] had fallen'. He has been killed in sober earnest, 'shot through the heart'. W.J. Roberts shows the scene on the stage with the red curtains drawn and Baker lying dead. Eve Turner as Coletta and a stage-hand look on.

Author of 'Poison in Play' (68th Thous)
HUTCHINSON

Death Goes on Skis

NANCY SPAIN

Hutchinson n.d. (1949)
artist: **unknown**

Death Goes on Skis is dedicated to Hermione Gingold, the model for its detective, Miriam Birdseye. It is set in Schizo-Frenia, somewhere in the Alps, among a party of British tourists, two of whom are murdered. The wrapper shows 'the cold stillness of a wrapped, white world', with 'the ski-lift creaking and groaning most distressingly' up or down the Lavahorn and, below, a solitary skier of vaguely Russian aspect. Two members of the party are sufficiently expert to appear solo in this manner: Barney Flaherté, who 'rushed seriously down the Ski Championship course, twice an hour, travelling like a bullet'; and Natasha DuVivien, who shoots 'down the Bumps like a hundred-pound shell', 'spanking along the straight to the ravine'.

The Flying Fifty-Five

EDGAR WALLACE

Hutchinson 1922
artist: **Doco**

William, Earl of Fontwell, a wealthy young nobleman, undertakes for a bet to walk to Scotland and back with only a shilling in his pocket. On his return journey, he is seen by Stella Barrington, who trains the horses left to her by her father. She mistakes him for a tramp and offers him work in her stables. As Bill Lord, he is able to frustrate the schemes of an unscrupulous enemy of Stella; and he also trains and rides the black colt, Fifty-five, for the Derby. The horse is 'second favourite and it might even win'. Doco's wrapper for Edgar Wallace's *The Flying Fifty-five* shows the colt on the Epsom racecourse, the Earl of Fontwell up.

EDGAR WALLACE
Author of "FOUR JUST MEN." etc.

Case with Ropes and Rings

LEO BRUCE

Nicholson & Watson 1940
artist: **Youngman Carter**

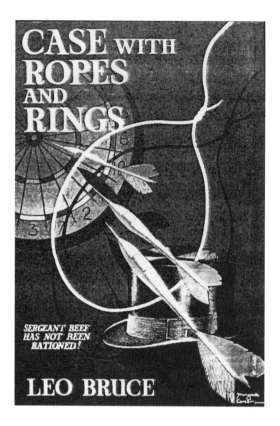

Case with Ropes and Rings gives Sergeant
Beef temporary employment as porter at
Penshurst School, where he investigates
the death of Lord Alan Foulkes, the
school's star boxer, who has been found
'hanging from a beam in the gymnasium'
the day after winning his title. The darts
and board on Youngman Carter's blue and
red wrapper remind us that Beef is also a
sportsman: 'a passionate darts-player',
though 'no champion': 'it was his fervour
that was remarkable, not his skill'. None
the less, he wins 'the "White Horse"
championship' playing 'extremely well'
and beating 'his opponent in a most
spectacular manner'. He also instals 'a dart
board on the door of the tall cupboard in
which his silk hat was kept'.

Gambit

REX STOUT

Collins Crime Club 1963
artist: **? John Rose**

Gambit involves Nero Wolfe with the
members of the Gambit Club, a New
York 'chess club with two floors in an old
brick building on West Twelfth Street'.
Paul Jerin dies in the course of the
'simultaneous blindfold games' he is
playing 'with twelve of the members'.
Matthew Blount has provided the only
refreshment taken by the dead man and so
becomes the natural suspect. At one point
Wolfe startles both Ernst Hausman and the
reader by responding to Hausman's
expressed with to play him at chess by
launching into a game without 'board or
men'. The white wrapper, in Rose's
characteristic style, has red chessmen and a
blue poison bottle.

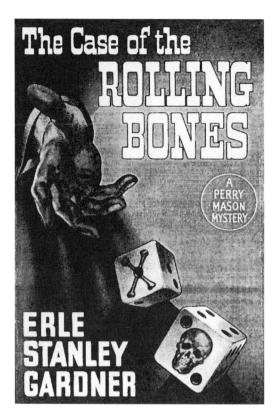

The Case of the Rolling Bones

ERLE STANLEY GARDNER

Cassell 1935
artist: **James E. McConnell**

In Erle Stanley Gardner's fourth novel, *The Case of the Rolling Bones*, relatives of millionaire Alden E. Leeds want him 'declared incompetent'. His niece Phyllis thinks her uncle is being blackmailed and asks Perry Mason to discover if this is true. Mason brings in detective Paul Drake to assist. Leeds, who has been taken to a sanatorium by his family, disappears, but is seen visiting the apartment of Louie Conway, to whom he has recently made out a $20,000 cheque. Conway is later found murdered. McConnell illustrates – in brown, grey and black on white – the merchandise supplied by the Conway Appliance Company. Drake, having drawn 'a pair of dice out of his pocket' throws them 'across the desk'. By rolling them, Mason establishes that they are 'loaded dice'.

The Casino Murder Case

S.S. VAN DINE

Scribner 1934
artist: **unknown**

The Casino Murder Case is the eighth of the 12 cases of the languid New York polymath known 'for purposes of anonymity' as Philo Vance. Such is his intellectual supremacy that the District Attorney of New York County turns to him whenever a case threatens difficulty beyond the ordinary; but on this occasion it is Vance who becomes involved first, by way of a letter from the murderer. The black wrapper has a green file card of the case, in the format common to most of the Vance series. It is enlivened by a roulette wheel with 'numbered compartments' of alternating red and black and 'the green area marked "O"' on which Vance is successful at Richard Kinkaid's Casino on West Seventy-third Street.

The Abbot's Cup

CYRIL ALINGTON

Herbert Jenkins 1930
artist: **De Groot**

The Abbot's Cup is the second of Cyril Alington's gentle mysteries, written in a sub-Wodehousean vein during his headmastership of Eton. The cup is the cherished heirloom of the Maresborough family and serves as focal point for a complicated narrative, in which it encounters various indignities. Dolly Rotherham sets the plot in motion by 'borrowing' the cup from his uncle to raise the money for a bridge debt: De Groot shows him in the process of losing £500 to the rich American, Marcus T. Hocking. The looming shadow of a man holding the cup is rather a sinister image for so lively a story.

The Body in the Library

AGATHA CHRISTIE

Collins Crime Club 1942
artist: **Leslie Stead**

The Body in the Library is that of a young platinum blonde who has been strangled. The library is at Gossington Hall in the quiet village of St Mary Mead, the home of Colonel and Mrs Bantry. The housemaid, Mary, discovers the body, having gone 'into the library … to draw the curtains'. Mrs Bantry immediately seeks the help of Miss Jane Marple, an old friend also resident in the village, as she is 'so good at bodies' and 'very good at murders'. Hitherto Dolly Bantry has believed that murders 'only happened in books'. Stead's clever wrapper design for this Agatha Christie novel is of black and white books arranged on three shelves, with the title picked out in red on the spines of the books.

Death off the Fairway

HERBERT ADAMS

Collins Crime Club 1936
artist: **C. Losin**

Basil Skelton is murdered in Herbert
Adams' *Death off the Fairway*: 'The gloved
hands held the body down … A faint
bubbling sound … A quick convulsive
movement … Soon all was over. The body
sagged lifeless in the stream.' Losin shows
us a very attractive view of the Burlesford
golf links in South Devon, with Roger
Bennion and Edna Hartwell walking
towards the 14th hole: 'The grass grew
down to the water's edge and they walked
slowly, looking for the little white object.
But it was another object that caught
Roger's eye … In the middle of the
stream, below the surface, yet half-afloat,
there was the fully clothed body of a man.'
The killer's attempt to make the murder
appear suicide is foiled by Roger Bennion,
who spots the one mistake that shows the
truth. [See colour section, page (l).]

A Bullet in the Ballet

CARYL BRAHMS AND S.J. SIMON

Joseph 1937
artist: **Bip Pares**

A Bullet in the Ballet is the first of the
Brahms and Simon novels and their nearest
approach to a true detective novel. Like its
successors, it is gay and amusing, with
running jokes, eccentric characters and
vivacious narrative. Inspector Adam Quill
investigates murder at the Ballet
Stroganoff, where successive Petroushkas
are shot while performing the role. Bip
Pares' wrapper faithfully depicts the corpse
of Anton Palook as described on the
opening page: 'Its white jumper is
scalloped with scarlet and jade. It wears a
yellow bouffon wig, a Russian clown's hat
and undertaker's gloves. It is bending over
the top of a booth, its arms swinging
limply over the sides.' [See colour section,
page (l).]

Death Is No Sportsman

CYRIL HARE

Faber 1938
artist: **Arthur Barbosa**

In Cyril Hare's *Death Is No Sportsman*, four
men compose a syndicate which gives
them 'the fishing rights of a reach of the
River Didder' and entitles them 'to cast a
fly upon those limpid waters'. The
members have beats 'assigned to them
throughout the fishing season in strict
rotation'. Barbosa's wrapper shows Jimmy
Rendel advancing up the bank of the
Didder, rod in hand, towards Sir Peter
Packer's stockinged legs, projecting from
the tall reeds round the tump. Packer has
had 'the back of his head blown off'. The
local police call in Scotland Yard, who
send Inspector Mallett to solve the case.
[See colour section, page (l).]

Gin and Murder

JOSEPHINE PULLEIN-THOMPSON

Hale 1959
artist: **Sax**

Gin and Murder is the first of three rural
whodunits by Josephine Pullein-
Thompson, a daughter of Joanna Cannan,
with whom she shares a certain crisp
elegance. She is known chiefly as a writer
of 'pony books' and horses figure
prominently in her detective fiction. Sax
wisely gives one prominence, together
with the West Wintshire hounds and a
male hunter, perhaps the Master of
Foxhounds, Mark Broughton, who finds
himself under siege as the chief suspect,
since he was jealous of the first victim and
was married to the alcoholic second.
Chief-Inspector James Flecker investigates,
as always: here he takes over from a ham-
fisted local detective. [See colour section,
page (l).]

18
Old Bones

Death Cuts a Silhouette

D.B. OLSEN

Doubleday Crime Club 1939
artist: **Leo Manso**

Death Cuts a Silhouette is the second of
D.B. Olsen's novels, a grim, dark story of
sexual tensions within a large family,
assembled for a 4th of July celebration.
One by one, the Eriksens sit for their
portraits in silhouette, cut by the family
coquette, who caricatures the women,
only 'enjoying her work' when 'it
concerned masculine material'. She has 'an
undoubted knack for the business', cutting
'busily, her scissors bright and quick'; but
her art is too explicit and her violent death
is one of the consequences. Manso's
wrapper features the skeleton at the feast,
wielding the scissors and itself producing a
silhouette.

Skeletons and Cupboards

RALPH ARNOLD

Heinemann 1952
artist: **C.W. Bacon**

Skeletons and Cupboards is the first of
Colonel Charles Chaplin's two recorded
cases. He is on hand when James Kent
Brisbane is murdered at Hinning Hall, the
seat of the Ellonbys. The victim has been
widely disliked and three earlier attempts
on his life have been made: a spirit-lamp
has been primed to explode in his face; a
trophy shield to fall on his head; and a
rope to give way when he puts his weight
on it. The Colonel asks about 'family
skeletons in the Ellonby cupboard' and is
assured that there are none. Events prove
otherwise, however. C.W. Bacon shows
the Ellonby skeleton in the act of
emerging from its confinement.

Post Mortem

GUY CULLINGFORD

Hammond 1953
artist: **Sax**

Post Mortem is a first-person narrative by
the minor novelist, Gilbert Worth, written,
as the title indicates, after his death. There
is nothing to suggest in the early stages of
the story that he is victim as well as
narrator, until a door is shut in his face and
he turns to see 'the man in the chair with
his head half blown away'. The realization
strikes him 'like a blow in the mouth': 'It
was myself.' Sax's dark, macabre wrapper
shows Gilbert's skeletal hands at work on
the manuscript, recording 'the exact
sequence of events' after finding himself
dead.

The Puzzle of the Happy Hooligan

STUART PALMER

Collins Crime Club 1941
artist: **Nicolson**

The Puzzle of the Happy Hooligan takes
Hildegarde Withers to Hollywood, where,
to her own amazement, she is employed
by Mammoth Pictures as a technical
adviser to the 'epic biography' of Lizzie
Borden. Soon after taking possession of her
office, she finds her neighbour 'sprawled
akimbo upon the carpet' with a broken
neck. She learns the murder method by
direct experience, all but succumbing to
'the terrible pressure' exerted by the killer's
hands on her own head. Nicolson's blue
wrapper makes thematic representation of
the studio disrupted by murder, with a
skeletal hand reaching towards a film
camera in silhouette.

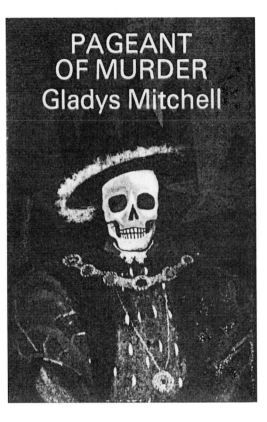

Pageant of Murder

GLADYS MITCHELL

Joseph 1965
artist: **Broom Lynne**

Pageant of Murder concerns a series of
'haywire and unnecessary' murders in a
small Thames-side town newly created a
borough. In celebration, a pageant is held,
with Kitty Trevelyan – from *Laurels Are
Poison* – as pageant-master. When actors in
the pageant are murdered in character
Dame Beatrice Bradley detects a bizarre
'common denominator': it is as if 'they
were shown up ... in the midst of their
sins'. Falstaff is dumped in the river and
Henry VIII is decapitated, perhaps in
revenge for Ann Boleyn. Broom Lynne's
opulent wrapper presents the standard
image of Henry VIII but with a grinning
skull instead of a face.

Say it with Flowers

GLADYS MITCHELL

Joseph 1960
artist: **Kenneth Farnhill**

Say it with Flowers finds Dame Beatrice
Bradley exactly in mid-career, with 33
cases behind her and 32 still to come. The
action begins with Dick Dickon's
discovery of Roman coins and pottery at
Wandles Parva, where Dame Beatrice
lives. Further excavation unearths a
complete skeleton with a split skull,
uncritically accepted as a relic of the
Roman occupation: in the words of the
local headmaster, 'everybody connects the
bones with the previous finds'. Dame
Beatrice knows better, however; and,
having 'subjected the bones to keen
scrutiny', she insists that they are recent.
Farnhill's wrapper, in characteristic style,
has Dickon's spade outlined against an
orange sky and the skull embedded in a
rich pink soil.

The House on the Hard

ANTHONY WYNNE

Hutchinson n.d. (1940)
artist: **unknown**

The House on the Hard is a late case for Dr Eustace Hailey, who initially investigates the disappearance of Miss Fairfax from her house at Sowley Hard on the Solent. There are bloodstains in her bedroom and the creeper outside her window shows signs of having been climbed: scars, snapped twigs and a blossom hanging 'pale and shrivelled by a strip of bark'. A 'huge wistaria' 'in full flower', it has 'spread itself all over the brickwork, veiling it and yet leaving it undiminished'. It features prominently on the anonymous pink wrapper, where it supports a cloaked and hooded skeleton, clawing its way up the wall with a dagger in its right hand.

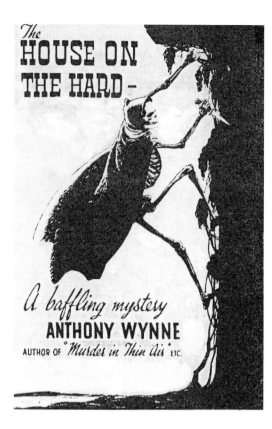

The Corpse Steps Out

CRAIG RICE

Eyre & Spottiswoode 1940
artist: **Freda Nichols**

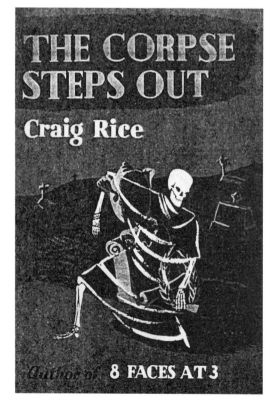

The Corpse Steps Out is set in Chicago, like most of the novels about John J. Malone, the city's 'noisiest and most successful lawyer'. Also involved are Jake Justus and Helen Brand, the latter for the last time in her maiden name. To protect from harmful publicity the popular radio singer who employs him as press agent, he moves both of the corpses he encounters, propping up the first 'beside the kitchen door' of John St John's apartment, and transferring the second from the radio building to a less suggestive park bench. Freda Nichols' lively wrapper has a blithe-looking skeleton in the act of stepping out from the cemetery.

The Skeleton in the Clock

CARTER DICKSON

Morrow 1948
artist: **Charles Lofgren**

The Skeleton in the Clock is found in the first bar parlour of the Dragon's Rest Inn, near Rimdown, Berkshire. Sir Henry Merrivale, Carter Dickson's regular detective, investigates a 20-year old case which takes him to the inn. Lofgren clearly presents what the text describes: the clock, standing 'in the angle of the wall, south-east, beyond the mantelpiece' and the 'tall curtains of heavy red velvet'. 'It was about six feet high, including its platform–base, and of dark polished wood, elaborately wrought at the top.' The 'skull-face' looks out with 'a smug look' from 'its dusky recess', through 'a round glass dial, with gilt numerals and hands'. 'The clock-case had another glass panel, oblong, so that you could see the skeleton behind a brass pendulum.'

Death on the Board

JOHN RHODE

Collins Crime Club 1937
artist: **unknown**

Death on the Board is the Dr Priestley novel in which the entire board of directors of a successful firm is murdered in sequence. Porslin Ltd deals in 'ironmongery of every description' and has a Holborn headquarters and 'branches in nearly every provincial town' that 'usually contrive to undersell their competitors'. The narrative advances grimly through the succession of deaths, as each board member is murdered in his turn: Sir Andrew Wigenhall in an explosion; his brother Percival by poison; Mr Grimshaw by gas; and Mr Tunstead and Colonel Flotman by burning. The bright red wrapper has a symbolic skeleton by the boardroom table at Porslin House.

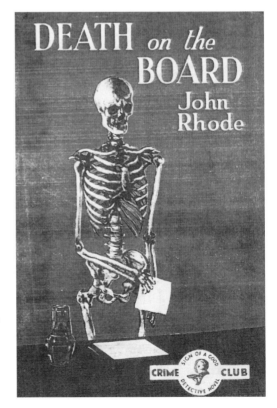

A Minor Operation

J.J. CONNINGTON

Hodder & Stoughton 1937
artist: **Thompson**

While Leonard Deerhurst is in jail, he makes his will. From that moment the sinister Shadow of Death is poised to take him as soon as he is released; as shown by Thompson standing at the centre of the blue and white wrapper for J.J. Connington's *A Minor Operation*. The prison window, the telegram which lures Deerhurst to his death and a curious machine all cleverly reflect aspects of the plot. Sir Clinton Driffield and his friend Squire Wendover investigate Deerhurst's murder and the disappearance of his wife Hazel. Wendover identifies the mysterious machine as a braille writer: 'a Stainsby ... with the keys arranged to correspond with the position of the dots in ordinary Braille type.'

Mr Fortune's Trials

H.C. BAILEY

Methuen 1925
artist: **Frank Wright**

Mr Fortune's Trials is the third of the Reggie Fortune collections, containing six long stories, of which one, 'The Hermit Crab', is comic. The others are deeper and darker. Two eras overlap in Frank Wright's wrapper, which illustrates 'The Profiteers', the last of the six and perhaps the most remarkable. He shows Sarah Herne, the tragic victim of a brutal seventeenth-century murder, and the last descendant of her murderer, John Douty junior, who dies 200 years later, 'by the vengeance of God'. Sarah's skull and bones lie between them, bridging the years between her time and his.

Cakes for your Birthday

C.E. VULLIAMY

Joseph 1959
artist: **Broom Lynne**

C.E. Vulliamy, in his own name and also as 'Anthony Rolls', produced ten witty inverted crime novels. In *Cakes for your Birthday*, three apparently respectable gentlemen decide that Miss Millicent Peaswillow is too bad to live any longer, so they set up a Liquidation Committee and plan to send her poisoned cakes for her birthday: 'A paste of lead arsenate is combined with ordinary sugar icing and the cakes ... are sent ... by post in a pretty little box with a birthday card ... What could be simpler?' Broom Lynne's mauve wrapper depicts in yellow, black and white the three members of the committee, each with his 'Old Rotters' tie which flowed out so splendidly' over his shirt, each with a hand on their intended victim's skull.

A Bone and a Hank of Hair

LEO BRUCE

Peter Davies 1961
artist: **Biro**

In *A Bone and a Hank of Hair*, Leo Bruce's detective, Carolus Deene, is asked by the relations of a Mrs Rathbone to investigate her disappearance. He soon realizes that he could be looking for a habitual wife murderer. We learn that Rathbone 'had been digging ... and in his perturbed state had forgotten to leave the garden fork outside' but had stood it 'in the hall'. Deene is advised to dig to find a victim and makes a gruesome discovery: 'It was a human skull ... like an old bone long buried by a dog, rotten and muddy and horrifying.' Biro's design is typical of the style he developed for ten of Bruce's books published by Peter Davies, each reflecting details of the text.

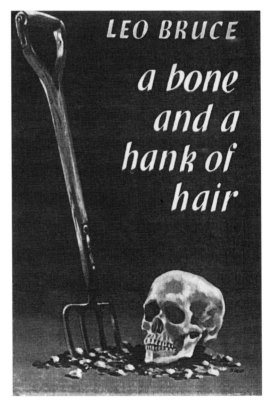

The Three Hunting Horns

MARY FITT

Nicholson & Watson 1937
artist: **Eugene Hastain**

The Three Hunting Horns introduces
Colonel Anderson, a minor Fitt detective
who recurs in a few later titles as
Superintendent Mallet's Chief Constable.
Moving here in French high society, he is
present at the Chateau de la Frelonnerie
when the Marquis and his brother die
within minutes of each other, each after
playing on a hunting horn. The
eponymous horns were 'made by skilled
craftsmen for kings and princes' and hang
on a wall in the Chateau: they are 'circular
... each with its faded green tassel'.
Hastain's thematic wrapper is akin to
others that he designed for Mary Fitt's
earliest phase, adapting a symbolic skeleton
to the milieu of the novel.

Murder Mars the Tour

MARY FITT

Nicholson & Watson 1936
artist: **Eugene Hastain**

Murder Mars the Tour is the second of Mary
Fitt's novels, set in the Austrian Tyrol,
where the members of the Quest Club are
walking for pleasure. In Vienna, they
encounter Elena Brain, the volatile wife of
an ugly older man, who entertains some of
the company the day before she is found
strangled. Hastain's striking wrapper is
dominated by a skeletal guide in Tyrolean
costume, with a group silhouette of
walkers ascending a slope. Beyond is the
'stupendous panorama' of the Austrian
mountains: 'the jagged ridges ... striped in
their summer garment of snow ... the
tremendous sides of rock sweeping down
to ravines and valleys'.

Artists in Crime

Certain artists made a significant contribution to the art of the crime fiction dustwrapper. The lists that follow give such details as we know of thirty whose work is reproduced in this book. All known dustwrapper designs are listed for each artist. Supplementary information is given where it is known.

Abbey

There are two Abbeys in the field: S. Abbey, whose work appeared in 'The Strand Magazine' and elsewhere, and J. Abbey, who illustrated books by Enid Blyton in the 1940s. S. Abbey is Salomon van Abbé (1883–1955), who signed work also in his own name and as 'C. Morse' (q.v.). J. Abbey is his younger brother Joseph, born in 1889. Salomon used the rounded capital 'A', Joseph the formal printed one.

Arthur Conan Doyle   HIS LAST BOW 1917; THE CASE-BOOK OF SHERLOCK HOLMES   1927 (both 'J. Abbey')
Dorothy L. Sayers   CLOUDS OF WITNESS 1926 ('J. Abbey')
Gordon Daviot   THE MAN IN THE QUEUE 1929 ('J. Abbey')

S. Abbey

Oliver Fleming   AMBROTOX AND LIMPING DICK 1920
J.S. Fletcher   SCARHAVEN KEEP 1920
E. Phillips Oppenheim   THE GREAT IMPERSONATION 1920
John Rhode   THE ELLERBY CASE 1927; TRAGEDY AT 'THE UNICORN' 1928

Leslie Charteris   THE WHITE RIDER 1928; THE BANDIT 1929; DAREDEVIL 1929
H.C. Bailey   MR. FORTUNE SPEAKING 1929; MR. FORTUNE EXPLAINS 1930
Herbert Adams   JOHN BRAND'S WILL 1933
John Dickson Carr   THE BURNING COURT 1937; THE CROOKED HINGE 1938; THE BLACK SPECTACLES 1939
F.J. Whaley   THIS PATH IS DANGEROUS 1939

V. Asta

G.D.H. & M. Cole   DEAD MAN'S WATCH 1931
Hulbert Footner   EASY TO KILL 1931
John Dickson Carr   THE WAXWORKS MURDER 1932; POISON IN JEST 1932
John Rhode   THE VENNER CRIME 1933; IN FACE OF THE VERDICT 1936
C. Daly King   OBELISTS EN ROUTE 1934
Roger East   DETECTIVES IN GUM-BOOTS 1936
Cyril Alington   CRIME ON THE KENNET 1939
Phoebe Atwood Taylor   THE ASEY MAYO TRIO 1946

J.Z. Atkinson

Atkinson also designed wrappers for mainstream novelists, e.g. Eric Linklater, E. Arnot Robertson.

Agatha Christie   TOWARDS ZERO 1944
A. Fielding   POINTER TO A CRIME 1944
E.C.R.Lorac   FELL MURDER 1944;
   CHECKMATE TO MURDER 1944

Arthur Barbosa

Barbosa was Georgette Heyer's designer for many years.

Cyril Hare   DEATH IS NO SPORTSMAN 1938
Lucy Cores   LET'S KILL GEORGE 1950
C.A. Alington   GOLD AND GAITERS 1950
Carter Dickson   FEAR IS THE SAME 1956

C.W. Bacon (1905–1992)

Cecil Walter Bacon worked in advertising and for the Ministry of Information (1942–6). He illustrated several books and published SCRAPERBOARD DRAWING in 1951.

Patricia Wentworth   SEVEN GREEN STONES 1933
Richard Hull   THE GHOST IT WAS 1937
Eden Phillpotts   MONKSHOOD 1939
Elspeth Huxley   DEATH OF AN ARYAN 1939
Gladys Mitchell   BRAZEN TONGUE 1940
Margery Allingham   TRAITOR'S PURSE 1941
Baynard Kendrick   DEATH KNELL 1946
Herbert Brean   WILDERS WALK AWAY 1949; HARDLY A MAN IS NOW ALIVE 1952
Raymond Chandler   THE LITTLE SISTER 1949
John Dickson Carr   BELOW SUSPICION 1950; THE NINE WRONG ANSWERS 1952; PATRICK BUTLER FOR THE DEFENCE 1956
Georgette Heyer   DUPLICATE DEATH 1951
Ralph Arnold FISH AND COMPANY 1951; SKELETONS AND CUPBOARDS 1952
Christopher Bush   THE CASE OF THE BURNT BOHEMIAN 1953; THE CASE OF THE RED BRUNETTE 1954

Austin Lee   MISS HOGG AND THE BRONTË MURDERS 1956
James Turner   THE DARK INDEX 1959
P.M. Hubbard COLD WATERS 1970

Biro (b. 1921)

Balint Stephen Biro is also known as Val Biro. Alan Horne states that he has illustrated 'some 400 books' (20th CENTURY BOOK ILLUSTRATORS, 1994).

Alice Tilton   THE HOLLOW CHEST 1942
A.A. Milne   BIRTHDAY PARTY   1949
F.V. Morley   DWELLY LANE 1952
Max Murray   THE DOCTOR AND THE CORPSE 1953; THE SUNSHINE CORPSE 1954; ROYAL BED FOR A CORPSE 1955
Sebastian Fox   OTHER MAN'S POISON 1956; ODD WOMAN OUT 1958
Leo Bruce   DEAD FOR A DUCAT 1956; DEAD MAN'S SHOES 1958; A LOUSE FOR THE HANGMAN 1958; OUR JUBILEE IS DEATH 1959; JACK ON THE GALLOWS TREE 1960; FURIOUS OLD WOMEN 1960; A BONE AND A HANK OF HAIR 1961; DIE ALL, DIE MERRILY 1961; NOTHING LIKE BLOOD 1962; CRACK OF DOOM 1963
John Dickson Carr   THE THIRD BULLET 1954; THE DEAD MAN'S KNOCK 1958; SCANDAL AT HIGH CHIMNEYS 1959; A DR. FELL OMNIBUS 1959; THE WITCH OF THE LOW TIDE 1961; THE DEMONIACS 1962; MOST SECRET 1964; THE MEN WHO EXPLAINED MIRACLES 1964

Youngman Carter (1904–1969)

Philip Youngman Carter was married to Margery Allingham. He designed wrappers for many mainstream novelists including E.F. Benson, Pearl S. Buck, Daphne du Maurier, Graham Greene, Georgette Heyer, J.B. Priestley, H.G. Wells and Rebecca West. He edited *The Tatler* and published two Albert Campion novels after his wife's death.

Margery Allingham   THE WHITE COTTAGE MYSTERY 1928; THE CRIME AT BLACK DUDLEY 1929;

MYSTERY MILE 1930; LOOK TO THE
LADY 1931; POLICE AT THE FUNERAL
1931; SWEET DANGER 1933; DEATH
OF A GHOST 1934; FLOWERS FOR
THE JUDGE 1936; DANCERS IN
MOURNING 1937; THE FASHION IN
SHROUDS 1938; MR. CAMPION AND
OTHERS 1939; BLACK PLUMES 1940;
THE TIGER IN THE SMOKE 1952; THE
BECKONING LADY 1955; HIDE MY
EYES 1958; THE CHINA GOVERNESS
1963; THE MYSTERIOUS MR.
CAMPION 1963; THE MIND READERS
1965; MR. CAMPION'S LADY 1965; MR.
CAMPION'S CLOWNS 1967; CARGO
OF EAGLES 1968; THE ALLINGHAM
CASEBOOK 1969
Christopher Bush   CUT THROAT 1932
E.C.R. Lorac   THE CASE OF COLONEL
MARCHAND 1933
G.D.H. & M. Cole   DEATH IN THE
QUARRY 1934; END OF AN ANCIENT
MARINER 1934
Carter Dickson   THE BOWSTRING
MURDERS 1934; THE MAGIC
LANTERN MURDERS 1936; THE
JUDAS WINDOW 1938; DEATH IN FIVE
BOXES 1938; DROP TO HIS DEATH
with John Rhode 1940
John Ferguson   THE GROUSE MOOR
MYSTERY 1934
John Rhode   POISON FOR ONE 1934;
THE ROBTHORNE MYSTERY 1934
Henry Wade   CONSTABLE GUARD
THYSELF! 1934
Val Gielgud   DEATH AS AN EXTRA 1935
Richard Keverne   CROOK STUFF 1935
Maxwell March (Margery Allingham)
ROGUES' HOLIDAY 1935; THE
SHADOW IN THE HOUSE 1936
Ethel Lina White   THE FIRST TIME HE
DIED 1935
Helen McCloy   DESIGN FOR DYING 1938
Clyde B. Clason   CLUE TO THE
LABYRINTH 1939; THE WHISPERING
EAR 1939
Gladys Mitchell   PRINTER'S ERROR 1939
Leo Bruce   CASE WITH ROPES AND
RINGS 1940
Shelley Smith   THE BALLAD OF THE
RUNNING MAN 1961

Georges Simenon   MAIGRET IN COURT
1961; MAIGRET AFRAID 1961
Raymond Chandler   THE SMELL OF FEAR
1965

Hookway Cowles

Cowles illustrated a number of classic adventure
novels between 1948 and 1965, including
eleven titles by H. Rider Haggard.

Richard Hull   THE MURDER OF MY
AUNT 1934; KEEP IT QUIET 1935; THE
MURDERERS OF MONTY 1937
John Dickson Carr   THE EMPEROR'S
SNUFFBOX 1943; TILL DEATH DO US
PART 1944; HE WHO WHISPERS 1946;
THE SLEEPING SPHINX 1947

Ellen Edwards

R. Austin Freeman   HELEN VARDON'S
CONFESSION 1922; THE SHADOW OF
THE WOLF 1925
Ernest Bramah   THE SPECIMEN CASE 1924
Lynn Brock   COLONEL GORE'S SECOND
CASE 1925
G.D.H. & M. Cole   DEATH OF A
MILLIONAIRE 1925
A. Fielding   THE CHARTERIS MYSTERY
1925
Hulbert Footner   THE UNDER DOGS 1925
J. Kilmeny Keith (Anthony Gilbert)   THE
MAN WHO WAS LONDON 1925
(Anthony Berkeley)   THE WYCHFORD
POISONING CASE 1926
Agatha Christie   THE MURDER OF
ROGER ACKROYD 1926
Elizabeth Daly   MURDERS IN VOLUME 2
1943

Kenneth Farnhill

Nancy Spain   POISON FOR TEACHER
1949; R IN THE MONTH 1950;
CINDERELLA GOES TO THE
MORGUE 1950; NOT WANTED ON
VOYAGE 1951; OUT DAMNED TOT
1952
Agatha Christie   MRS. McGINTY'S DEAD
1952; THEY DO IT WITH MIRRORS
1952; HICKORY DICKORY DOCK 1955;
THIRD GIRL 1966; ENDLESS NIGHT

1967; BY THE PRICKING OF MY
THUMBS 1968

Gladys Mitchell   THE TWENTY-THIRD
MAN 1957; SPOTTED HEMLOCK 1958;
THE MAN WHO GREW TOMATOES
1959; SAY IT WITH FLOWERS 1960;
THE NODDING CANARIES 1961; MY
BONES WILL KEEP 1962; ADDERS ON
THE HEATH 1963

Barbara Worsley-Gough   LANTERN HILL
1957

Ngaio Marsh   HAND IN GLOVE 1962;
DEAD WATER 1964; DEATH AT THE
DOLPHIN 1967; CLUTCH OF
CONSTABLES 1968

P.M. Hubbard   FLUSH AS MAY 1963;
PICTURE OF MILLIE 1964

Rex Stout   A RIGHT TO DIE 1965;
DEATH OF A DOXY 1967; DEATH OF A
DUDE 1970

Sara Woods   THE WINDY SIDE OF THE
LAW 1965; ENTER CERTAIN
MURDERERS 1966; THE CASE IS
ALTERED 1967

Ellis Peters   PIPER ON THE MOUNTAIN
1966; BLACK IS THE COLOUR OF MY
TRUE LOVE'S HEART 1967

D.M. Devine/Dominic Devine   THE FIFTH
CORD 1967; THE SLEEPING TIGER
1968

Nigel FitzGerald   AFFAIRS OF DEATH 1967

Joan Fleming   NO BONES ABOUT IT 1967;
KILL OR CURE 1968

Patricia Moyes   MURDER FANTASTICAL
1967

Val Gielgud   A NECESSARY END 1969

Julian Symons   THE MAN WHO LOST HIS
WIFE 1970

Eugène Hastain

R. Austin Freeman   THE PUZZLE LOCK
1925

Patricia Wentworth   GREY MASK 1928;
KINGDOM LOST 1931

Anthony Berkeley   TOP STOREY
MURDER 1931

Detection Club   THE FLOATING
ADMIRAL 1931

Roger East   MURDER REHEARSAL 1933

John Rhode   SHOT AT DAWN 1934

Ethel Lina White   WAX 1935

Mary Fitt   THREE SISTERS FLEW HOME
1936; MURDER MARS THE TOUR
1936; BULLS LIKE DEATH 1937; THE
THREE HUNTING HORNS 1937

Alex Jardine

Christopher Bush   THE CASE OF THE
BONFIRE BODY 1936

C. St John Sprigg   THE SIX QUEER
THINGS 1937

E.C.R. Lorac   THESE NAMES MAKE
CLUES 1937

G.D.H. & M. Cole   MRS. WARRENDER'S
PROFESSION 1938

Phoebe Atwood Taylor   OCTAGON
HOUSE 1938

Jolyon Carr (Ellis Peters)   FREEDOM FOR
TWO 1939

Miles Burton   MURDER OUT OF
SCHOOL 1951

Jarvis

Michael Gilbert   DEATH HAS DEEP
ROOTS 1951

Delano Ames   THE BODY ON PAGE ONE
1951; MURDER, MAESTRO, PLEASE
1952;

NO MOURNING FOR THE MATADOR
1953; LANDSCAPE WITH CORPSE 1955;
CRIME OUT OF MIND 1956

Patricia Wentworth   THE IVORY DAGGER
1953; ANNA, WHERE ARE YOU? 1953;
THE WATERSPLASH 1953; LADIES'
BANE 1954; OUT OF THE PAST 1955;
VANISHING POINT 1955; THE
BENEVENT TREASURE 1956; THE
LISTENING EYE 1957; THE GAZEBO
1958; THE FINGERPRINT 1959

John Sherwood   TWO DIED IN
SINGAPORE 1954

Freeman Wills Crofts   ANYTHING TO
DECLARE? 1957

Crime Writers Association   CHOICE OF
WEAPONS 1958; PLANNED
DEPARTURES 1958

Broom Lynne

James Broom Lynne is a writer as well as an

artist.

Mary Fitt   A FINE AND PRIVATE PLACE
1947; DEATH AND THE BRIGHT DAY
1948; THE BANQUET CEASES 1949; AN
ILL WIND 1951; DEATH AND THE
SHORTEST DAY 1952; THE
NIGHTWATCHMAN'S FRIEND 1953;
THE MAN WHO SHOT BIRDS 1954;
LOVE FROM ELIZABETH 1954; SWEET
POISON 1956
Edith Pargeter (Ellis Peters)   FALLEN INTO
THE PIT 1951
John Trench   DOCKEN DEAD 1953;
DISHONOURED BONES 1954
Helen Robertson   THE WINGED
WITNESSES 1955; VENICE OF THE
BLACK SEA 1956; THE CHINESE
GOOSE 1960
Christianna Brand   THE THREE-
CORNERED HALO 1957
Matthew Head   MURDER AT THE FLEA
CLUB 1957
C.E. Vulliamy   CAKES FOR YOUR
BIRTHDAY 1959; JUSTICE FOR JUDY
1960; TEA AT THE ABBEY 1961;
FLORAL TRIBUTE 1963
Mary Kelly   THE SPOILT KILL 1961; DUE
TO A DEATH 1962; MARCH TO THE
GALLOWS 1964; DEAD CORSE 1966
Jennie Melville (Gwendoline Butler)   COME
HOME AND BE KILLED 1962;
BURNING IS A SUBSTITUTE FOR
LOVING 1963; MURDERERS' HOUSES
1964; THERE LIES YOUR LOVE 1965
Gladys Mitchell   DEATH OF A DELFT
BLUE 1964; PAGEANT OF MURDER
1965; THE CROAKING RAVEN 1966;
SKELETON ISLAND 1967

Frank Marston

Herbert Adams   THE SECRET OF BOGEY
HOUSE 1924; THE SLOANE SQUARE
MYSTERY 1925; THE QUEEN'S GATE
MYSTERY 1927; THE EMPTY BED 1928;
ROGUES FALL OUT 1928; CAROLINE
ORMSBY'S CRIME 1929; ODDWAYS
1930
Leslie Charteris   X ESQUIRE 1927
Ronald A. Knox   THE FOOTSTEPS AT
THE LOCK 1927

Denis McLoughlin

McLoughlin is celebrated for the long series of
wrappers he designed for the 'Bloodhound'
series, published by Boardman from 1950 to the
1960s. There are many more titles than the few
listed here.

P.W. Wilson   BRIDE'S CASTLE 1946;
BLACK TARN 1948
Craig Rice   THE SUNDAY PIGEON
MURDERS 1948 (Nicholson & Watson)
Louisa Revell   THE BUS STATION
MURDERS 1949; NO POCKETS IN
SHROUDS 1949; A SILVER SPADE 1950;
THE KINDEST USE A KNIFE 1953
Ed McBain   COP HATER 1958; THE
MUGGER 1959

G.P. Micklewright

Rufus King   CRIME OF VIOLENCE 1938
Baynard Kendrick   THE LAST EXPRESS
1938; THE IRON SPIDERS 1938; THE
ODOUR OF VIOLETS 1941
Helen McCloy   SHE WALKS ALONE 1950

C. Morse (i.e. Salomon van Abbé (1883–1955))

According to Brigid Peppin and Lucy
Micklethwait (DICTIONARY OF BRITISH
BOOK ILLUSTRATORS; THE
TWENTIETH CENTURY, 1983) 'C. Morse'
is an alias of Salomon van Abbé, well
established as a graphic artist in his own name
and as 'S. Abbey' (q.v.).

Dorothy L. Sayers WHOSE BODY? 1923
Freeman Wills Crofts   THE GROOTE
PARK MURDERS 1923; INSPECTOR
FRENCH AND THE CHEYNE
MYSTERY 1926; INSPECTOR FRENCH
AND THE STARVEL TRAGEDY 1927
A. Fielding   DEEP CURRENTS 1924; THE
FOOTSTEPS THAT STOPPED 1926;
THE CLIFFORD AFFAIR 1927; THE
NET AROUND JOAN INGILBY 1928
Eden Phillpotts THE MARYLEBONE MISER
1926
Agatha Christie   THE MYSTERY OF THE
BLUE TRAIN 1928

J. Morton-Sale (1901–   )

John Morton-Sale worked in collaboration with his wife Isobel, illustrating a number of children's books, including several by Eleanor Farjeon. All known wrappers are signed by him alone.

G.D.H. & M. Cole   THE MAN FROM THE RIVER 1928

Henry Wade   THE DUKE OF YORK'S STEPS 1929

Clemence Dane & Helen Simpson PRINTER'S DEVIL 1930

E.C.R. Lorac   THE MURDER ON THE BURROWS 1931

Freeman Wills Crofts   FATAL VENTURE 1939

Clifford Witting   MEASURE FOR MURDER 1941

Elizabeth Ferrars DEATH IN BOTANIST'S BAY 1941; YOUR NECK IN A NOOSE 1942

E.H. Clements   PERHAPS A LITTLE DANGER 1942; BERRY GREEN 1945

Freda Nichols

Craig Rice   THE CORPSE STEPS OUT 1940

Gladys Mitchell   TOM BROWN'S BODY 1949; GROANING SPINNEY 1950

Max Murray   THE KING AND THE CORPSE 1949; NO DUTY ON A CORPSE 1950; THE NEAT LITTLE CORPSE 1951; THE RIGHT HONOURABLE CORPSE 1952

Jonathan Stagge   THE THREE FEARS 1949

Christianna Brand   LONDON PARTICULAR 1952; TOUR DE FORCE 1955

C.E. Vulliamy   DON AMONG THE DEAD MEN 1952

Barbara Worsley-Gough   ALIBI INNINGS 1954

Clara Stone   DEATH IN CRANFORD 1959

Nick, later Nicholson

In the 1920s and earlier 1930s, this artist was signing himself 'Nick' but by the end of the 1930s he had become 'Nicolson'.

Lynn Brock   THE DEDUCTIONS OF

COLONEL GORE 1924

J.S. Fletcher   THE CARTWRIGHT GARDENS MURDER 1924; MURDER AT WRIDES PARK 1931; MURDER IN THE SQUIRE'S PEW 1932

Philip MacDonald   THE RASP 1924

Eden Phillpotts   A VOICE FROM THE DARK 1925

A.B. Cox   MR. PRIESTLEY'S PROBLEM 1927

John Rhode   THE DAVIDSON CASE 1928

Anthony Wynne   THE ROOM WITH THE IRON SHUTTERS 1929

Christopher Bush   MURDER AT FENWOLD 1930; DANCING DEATH 1931; DEAD MAN TWICE 1932; THE CASE OF THE CHINESE GONG 1935

Stuart Palmer MURDER ON THE BLACKBOARD 1934; THE PUZZLE OF THE HAPPY HOOLIGAN 1941

Josephine Tey   A SHILLING FOR CANDLES 1936

Anthony Berkeley   TRIAL AND ERROR 1937

Patricia Wentworth   MR. ZERO 1938, RUN! 1938; LONESOME ROAD 1939; WHO PAYS THE PIPER 1940; DANGER POINT 1942; THE CHINESE SHAWL 1943; THE KEY 1946; LATTER END 1949; MISS SILVER COMES TO STAY 1951

J.J. Connington   THE COUNSELLOR 1939; THE FOUR DEFENCES 1940; NO PAST IS DEAD 1942; JACK IN THE BOX 1944; COMMONSENSE IS ALL YOU NEED 1947

Clifford Witting   CATT OUT OF THE BAG 1939

Dorothy Bowers   A DEED WITHOUT A NAME 1940

Val Gielgud   BEYOND DOVER 1940

Rupert Penny   SWEET POISON 1940

Rex Stout   DOUBLE FOR DEATH 1940

Miles Burton   DEATH OF TWO BROTHERS 1941

Gladys Mitchell   HANGMAN'S CURFEW 1941

Freeman Wills Crofts   DEATH OF A TRAIN 1946; SILENCE FOR THE MURDERER 1949

Jonathan Stagge   DEATH AND THE DEAR

GIRLS 1946

Delano Ames   SHE SHALL HAVE MURDER 1948; MURDER BEGINS AT HOME 1949; DEATH OF A FELLOW TRAVELLER 1950

Bip Pares

Ronald A. Knox   THE BODY IN THE SILO 1932; STILL DEAD 1934; DOUBLE CROSS PURPOSES 1937

Caryl Brahms & S.J. Simon   A BULLET IN THE BALLET 1937

Val Gielgud   DEATH IN BUDAPEST 1937

E.H. Clements   MAKE FAME A MONSTER 1940

Sheila Pim   CREEPING VENOM 1946

Freeman Wills Crofts   MURDERERS MAKE MISTAKES 1947

Michael Gilbert   CLOSE QUARTERS 1947; THEY NEVER LOOKED INSIDE 1948; THE DOORS OPEN 1949

John Sherwood   DISAPPEARANCE OF DR. BRUDERSTEIN 1949

William Randell

Miles Burton   MURDER UNRECOGNISED 1955; A CRIME IN TIME 1955; FOUND DROWNED 1956; DEATH IN A DUFFLE COAT 1956; MOTH-WATCH MURDER 1957; THE CHINESE PUZZLE 1957; BONES IN THE BRICKFIELD 1958; DEATH TAKES A DETOUR 1958; RETURN FROM THE DEAD 1959; A SMELL OF SMOKE 1959; LEGACY OF DEATH 1960; DEATH PAINTS A PICTURE 1960

Leslie Ford   INVITATION TO MURDER 1955

Rex Stout   THE BLACK MOUNTAIN 1955; THREE MEN OUT 1955; THREE WITNESSES 1956; IF DEATH EVER SLEPT 1958; THREE FOR THE CHAIR 1958; CRIME AND AGAIN 1959; THREE AT WOLFE'S DOOR 1961

Carol Carnac   THE DOUBLE TURN 1956; THE BURNING QUESTION 1957; LONG SHADOWS 1958; DEATH OF A LADY KILLER 1959

Nigel FitzGerald   IMAGINE A MAN 1956; THE STUDENT BODY 1958; THIS WON'T HURT YOU 1959

E.C.R. Lorac   MURDER IN VIENNA 1956; PICTURE OF DEATH 1957; DANGEROUS DOMICILE 1957; MURDER ON A MONUMENT 1958; DISHONOUR AMONG THIEVES 1959

Joan Fleming   YOU CAN'T BELIEVE YOUR EYES 1957; MALICE MATRIMONIAL 1959

Ellis Peters   DEATH MASK 1959; THE WILL AND THE DEED 1960

Beverley Nichols   MURDER BY REQUEST 1960

Ruth Rendell   FROM DOON WITH DEATH 1964; TO FEAR A PAINTED DEVIL 1965; VANITY DIES HARD 1966; A NEW LEASE OF DEATH 1967; WOLF TO THE SLAUGHTER 1967; THE SECRET HOUSE OF DEATH 1968; THE BEST MAN TO DIE 1969

Victor Reinganum (1907–1995)

Reinganum's work includes many drawings for the *Radio Times* and the dustwrapper designs for eight of Muriel Spark's books.

Richard Hull   MURDER ISN'T EASY 1936

Cyril Hare   TENANT FOR DEATH 1937; SUICIDE EXCEPTED 1939; WHEN THE WIND BLOWS 1949

Josephine Bell   DEATH ON THE RESERVE 1966

Robb

This artist is evidently different from Brian Robb (1913–1979), a prolific illustrator from the 1940s on.

John Rhode   THE HOUSE ON TOLLARD RIDGE 1929

Arthur Upfield   THE BEACH OF ATONEMENT 1930

Victor L. Whitechurch   MURDER AT THE PAGEANT 1930

Martin Porlock (Philip MacDonald)   MYSTERY AT FRIAR'S PARDON 1931

Sax

Sax designed wrappers for P.G. Wodehouse and illustrated the Popular Book Club edition of his

FRENCH LEAVE in 1957.

Pamela Branch   LION IN THE CELLAR 1951; MURDER EVERY MONDAY 1954; MURDER'S LITTLE SISTER 1958

Elizabeth Daly   THE BOOK OF THE LION 1951

Craig Rice   THE FOURTH POSTMAN 1951; THE DOUBLE FRAME 1958; MY KINGDOM FOR A HEARSE 1959; THE NAME IS MALONE 1960

Margaret Erskine DEATH OF OUR DEAR ONE 1952; DEAD BY NOW 1953; FATAL RELATIONS 1955

Guy Cullingford   POST MORTEM 1953; CONJURER'S COFFIN 1954; FRAMED FOR HANGING 1956; THE WHIPPING BOYS 1958; A TOUCH OF DRAMA 1960

Roy Vickers   EIGHT MURDERS IN THE SUBURBS 1954

Philip MacDonald   GUEST IN THE HOUSE 1956

S.H. Courtier   COME BACK TO MURDER 1957

Austin Lee   MISS HOGG AND THE SQUASH CLUB MURDER 1957

Joanna Pullein-Thompson   GIN AND MURDER 1959

Leslie L(eonard) Stead (1899–1966)

Alan Horne states (op. cit.) that between 1942 and 1965 Stead illustrated more than ninety books by W.E. Johns, the creator of Biggles.

Victor L. Whitechurch   THE TEMPLETON CASE 1924

R.A.J. Walling   THE FATAL FIVE MINUTES 1932; BURY HIM DEEPER 1937; THE CORONER DOUBTS 1938; MORE THAN ONE SERPENT 1938; DUST IN THE VAULT 1939; BY HOOK OR BY CROOK 1941; CASTLE-DINAS 1942

R. Austin Freeman   FOR THE DEFENCE; DR. THORNDYKE 1934

Patricia Wentworth   FEAR BY NIGHT 1934

Cecil M. Wills   FATAL ACCIDENT 1936

E.H. Clements   LET HIM DIE 1939

Georgette Heyer   NO WIND OF BLAME 1939; ENVIOUS CASCA 1941

E.C.R. Lorac   TRYST FOR A TRAGEDY 1940; CASE IN THE CLINIC 1941; ROPE'S END, ROGUE'S END 1942; THE SIXTEENTH STAIR 1942; DEATH CAME SOFTLY 1943; STILL WATERS 1949

Miles Burton   UP THE GARDEN PATH 1941; DEATH TAKES THE LIVING 1949

Dorothy Bowers   FEAR FOR MISS BETONY 1941

G.D.H. & M. Cole   KNIFE IN THE DARK 1941

Anthony Gilbert   THE WOMAN IN RED 1941; DEATH KNOCKS THREE TIMES 1949

Ngaio Marsh   SURFEIT OF LAMPREYS 1941; DEATH AND THE DANCING FOOTMAN 1942

Agatha Christie   THE BODY IN THE LIBRARY 1942; SPARKLING CYANIDE 1945

Phoebe Atwood Taylor   THE PERENNIAL BOARDER 1942

Leslie Ford   THE PHILADELPHIA MURDER STORY 1945

Clifford Witting   SUBJECT - MURDER 1945

A.E.W. Mason   THE HOUSE IN LORDSHIP LANE 1946

Stuart Palmer   FOUR LOST LADIES 1950

Stein

H.C. Bailey   THE WRONG MAN 1946; THE LIFE SENTENCE 1946; HONOUR AMONG THIEVES 1947; SAVING A ROPE 1948; SHROUDED DEATH 1950

Douglas G. Browne   TOO MANY COUSINS 1946; WHAT BECKONING GHOST 1947; SERGEANT DEATH 1955; DEATH IN SEVEN VOLUMES 1958

Christopher Bush   THE CASE OF THE MISSING MEN 1946

Carol Carnac   THE STRIPED SUITCASE 1946; CLUE SINISTER 1947; OVER THE GARDEN WALL 1948; UPSTAIRS, DOWNSTAIRS 1950; COPY FOR CRIME 1950

Herbert Adams   DIAMONDS ARE TRUMPS 1947; CRIME WAVE AT LITTLE CORNFORD 1948; ONE TO

PLAY 1949; THE DEAN'S DAUGHTERS 1950; EXIT THE SKELETON 1952; THE SPECTRE IN BROWN 1953; SLIPPERY DICK 1954; DEATH ON THE FIRST TEE 1957

Margaret Erskine   THE WHISPERING HOUSE 1947; I KNEW MACBEAN 1948; GIVE UP THE GHOST 1949; THE DISAPPEARING BRIDEGROOM 1950

Kathleen Freeman (Mary Fitt) GOWN AND SHROUD 1947

Selwyn Jepson   MAN RUNNING 1948; THE GOLDEN DART 1949; THE HUNGRY SPIDER 1951

C.H.B. Kitchin   THE CORNISH FOX 1949

Lange Lewis   MEAT FOR MURDER 1950

Carter Dickson   NIGHT AT THE MOCKING WIDOW 1951; BEHIND THE CRIMSON BLIND 1952; THE CAVALIER'S CUP 1954

E.H. Clements   OVER AND DONE WITH 1952

Joan Fleming   THE GOOD AND THE BAD 1953; THE DEEDS OF DR. DEADCERT 1955; HE OUGHT TO BE SHOT 1955

Georgette Heyer   DETECTION UNLIMITED 1953

Kenneth Hopkins   SHE DIED BECAUSE . . . 1957; THE FORTY-FIRST PASSENGER 1958; DEAD AGAINST MY PRINCIPLES 1960; PIERCE WITH A PIN 1960; BODY BLOW 1962; CAMPUS CORPSE 1963

Mystery Writers of America   CRIME FOR TWO 1957; FOR TOMORROW WE DIE 1958; A CHOICE OF MURDERS 1960

Dorothy Salisbury Davis   DEATH OF AN OLD SINNER 1958

Mary Fitt   CASE FOR THE DEFENCE 1958

Mary Kelly   THE CHRISTMAS EGG 1958

Austin Lee   MISS HOGG AND THE MISSING SISTERS 1961

Thompson

J.J. Connington   A MINOR OPERATION 1937; THE TWENTY-ONE CLUES 1941

Elizabeth Ferrars   GIVE A CORPSE A BAD NAME 1940; REMOVE THE BODIES 1940

Nicholas Blake   THE CASE OF THE ABOMINABLE SNOWMAN 1941

Agatha Christie   N OR M? 1941

John Rhode   THEY WATCHED BY NIGHT 1941

Rex Stout   RED THREADS 1941

Anthony Gilbert   SOMETHING NASTY IN THE WOODSHED 1942; THE CASE OF THE TEA-COSY'S AUNT 1942

Frank Wright

H.C. Bailey   CALL MR. FORTUNE 1920; MR. FORTUNE'S PRACTICE 1923; MR. FORTUNE'S TRIALS 1925

A.A. Milne   THE RED HOUSE MYSTERY 1922

Patricia Wentworth   THE ANNAM JEWEL 1924; THE RED LACQUER CASE 1924

Herbert Adams   BY ORDER OF THE FIVE 1925

Index of Artists

(**Note:** Speculative attributions are not included in this list.)

Index of Authors